# Raising Catholic Children

## Mary Ann Kuharski

Our Sunday Visitor Publishing Division
Our Sunday Visitor, Inc.
Huntington, IN 46750

Our Sunday Visitor Publishing Division
Our Sunday Visitor, Inc.
200 Noll Plaza
Huntington, Indiana 46750

ISBN: 0-87973-462-0
LCCCN: 91-60010

PRINTED IN THE UNITED STATES OF AMERICA

Cover design by Rebecca J. Heaston

462

To my husband, John, who has the patience of Job; to my children who are slowly but surely teaching me patience; to my parents and teachers who taught me faith and love; and to my extended family and friends, all of whom help me see the love of Jesus in every thing and every one

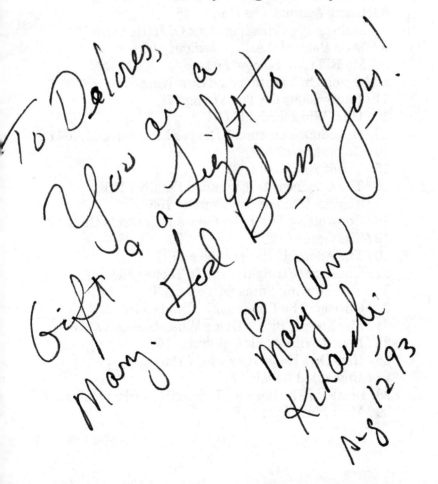

# Table of Contents

## Introduction

# Mom's Memoirs

Ever wish you'd taken notes or kept a journal as your kids were growing up? Realistically, most of us don't go around with pencils poised, waiting to capture those cute comments or more memorable moments.

As the mother of thirteen children, there have been times when I've had all I could do to keep a supply of dry diapers, much less a stash of clean paper — other than the kind that comes off a roll. Finding a pencil where the lead isn't broken off the top is an even greater challenge!

Over the years, however, I have managed to jot down some of the funny, if not unforgettable, happenings in our family. I would throw my little "precious moments" in a file folder marked "Mom's Memoirs," and as our children grew, I would occasionally look back or add footnotes to those tender times.

Granted, the memoir file would mean little to the casual onlooker. But to family, each memento recaptured is a treasure to recall.

I still chuckle when I recall the day our Tim (age seven) marched in the back door and asked, "Why can't our dad have a job as exciting as Dean's dad?" When I asked him what Dean's dad did, he replied, "Dean's dad is a magician."

"A magician in working-class Northeast Minneapolis?" I asked. "Well where does he do his magic tricks?"

"In a garage," Tim responded.

"Tim, I think Dean's dad is a mechanic, not a magician," I concluded with some relief. "I'm sure he fixes cars just as well as your dad works in an office as an accountant!"

Our Tim, we were to learn, had his own impression of just how archaic his parents were compared to modern day times. When assigned the task of describing "What it was like when my dad was in the Third grade," Tim's third-grade piece, pasted for all to see on the school hall wall, declared:

"When my Dad was in third grade, they did not have playground equipment or swing sets. The desks were all stuck together and they didn't have a chalk board. They didn't have lightbulbs. They didn't have pens. They had to write with feathers." (Not the kind of testimony a dad wants to see if he's just hit a landmark birthday or suddenly noticed his receding hairline has receded even more.)

I remember one of our first summer outings at grandma's lake cabin and the little old lady at the local grocery mart, who saw ten of our children, with their varied races and colors, pile out of the van. She rushed over and sweetly inquired, "Are they from Camp Courage or Camp Friendship?" — the two local summer camps for needy children. When I informed her that, "No. We are all one family," she backed away in shock. It never dawned on me that she probably thought each had a different father!

Pregnancy is always an interesting sex education opportunity at our house. These are a few of the comments and questions we've heard over the years:

"How do they tell if it's a boy or girl? Do they hook a machine up to the baby after it's born?"

"Can he stand on his head inside you?" "How about somersaults?"

"Will the baby always come out pink, just 'cus you and Daddy are pink?"

"How does the pizza you're eating get through the *biblical* cord to the baby?"

"What if there's a fire?"

"What if our new baby doesn't like it here?" Hmmmmmmmm.

At evening prayers: "Dear God, help our baby want to come out soon. Help Mommy have *fun* in the hospital."

Bringing home a new baby from the hospital always elicits some treasured thoughts:

At evening prayers:

"Thank you, Jesus, for our new baby. Even if he is a boy!"

"Do babies know what time it is?"

"When can we give him pizza."

"Are all babies this bald?"

"Wait till he finds out how many kids we got."

"How come they have fingernails but no hair?"

"Wait till Santa hears we gots another kid!"

"When will you be a Grandma?" EEEk!

On breastfeeding:

"Why can't daddy nurse the baby?"

"What do the moms do who have three babies?"

"Is one for chocolate, and one for white milk?"

"Doesn't he ever get bored — just nursin' all day?"

The addition by adoption of six children to our seven "tummy" kids, brought its own kind of hilarity as our children groped to understand the changes in our family size — or better still — tried to explain it to others.

There was the time we confided to our youngsters that mom was expecting and later learned that our Charlie, then twelve, announced the upcoming arrival in his Social Studies Class as part of their "Current Events News of the Day." (So much for family secrets!)

As zealously and carefully as we were to tell our young about their own beginnings and roots, and how we believed God had planned each of them and placed each one in our care, we have more than once been surprised to learn that some of our adopteds thought they were "tummy" products, and a couple of our "tummy" kids were convinced they were adopted. This would not seem unusual except for the fact that our six "imports" by adoption are all of mixed-races, four of whom came from foreign countries!

Once, Tony (then five), our Vietnamese son, asked, "Which ones of us are adopted?"

After we carefully explained to our roomful of young on-lookers, our Charlie, (then eight), a black Cambodian asked, "Well, which of us are Italian?"

We've learned that the difference in race and color goes unnoticed by young children. They are far more interested in character, courtesy, and kindness. I remember the evening we were all sitting at our picnic-sized dinner table, and young Kari (age four) blurted out as she looked over her plate to Charlie who sat across from her, "Hey, did you guys ever notice that Chawee (Charlie) has a really black face?"

We wanted our children to know that God has two ways of bringing families together: by tummy and by adoption. It was important that they saw adoption as being just as special and good as being "homespun."

It took a while before our children realized that not every family adopts children — especially children from varied countries and races. Charlie was about eight when he came in the door from Sunday Mass one day and asked, "Did you ever notice how some kids look just like their parents?"

Our Philippine born, Tina, was six when we moved into our big house on Pahl Avenue. She burst in the door on moving day and announced, "Guess what? There's a family with eight kids down the block and not one of them is adopted."

We adults often make much of "race relations." One year our Chrissy, then an enthusiastic six-year-old, asked to take her recently adopted, baby brother to school for show and tell. "Oh," I asked, "Did you want to tell everyone about his being adopted and coming all the way to our family from Vietnam?"

"Oh no, mama," Chrissy replied, "I don't care about that. I just wanted everyone to see him 'cus he's so cute; and besides yesterday Melissa brought her cat, so I thought I'd like to bring my baby brother."

Today's world is one of constant motion and frantic frenzy. Many people are searching for love and tenderness —

but in all the wrong places. Perhaps a "Memory file" of little loved ones' sayings will do nothing more than serve to remind us big people that it is only our faith, family, and friends, that help us sort the meaningless from the meaningful.

Have you a memory bank?

# Chapter 1

# Something More in Store

Our introduction to parenthood began naively for John and I in June 1968, with the birth of our first child, Christine Ann. My husband and I made an interesting pair. John was calm and collected and I was petrified.

What a shock. I think I cried the first three months over this colicky and new little fuss budget. I had thought babies were supposed to "sleep all the time."

The career of motherhood did not come naturally. I second-guessed everything I did. If I wasn't calling my mother or John's for advice, I was running to my pediatrician, or frantically checking the latest parenting books for the most up-to-date "tips" on mothering (usually written by "experts" who were childless themselves). Fortunately, it took only a matter of months before the books so thoroughly confused me that I trashed them all and went with prayer and common sense — which is the best advice I can give any new parent.

Yes, novices we were. Yet in spite of our jitters and baby's colicky crying, something was happening to us. We were falling in LOVE. What joy this seven-pound bundle of wet diapers had become to our already happy existence.

She made it worthwhile to "go without" or to "save for the future." Sweet, bright, and beautiful — each new day seemed to unfold another "first" in her young life and we were just happy to be part of it all. Johnny could hardly wait to get home from work each night. He'd bound through the door, plant a peck on my check and head straight for the baby. She seemed to draw us even closer in some mysterious way, as we shared in her discoveries, firsts, and growth.

In a very real sense, it was Chrissy, our irresistible little "first," that made us yearn for another. It was she who coaxed us on to what would become, an exciting, enthralling, energy-sapping, yet wonderful, adventure.

Chrissy, once a captivating, pig-tailed, joy-filled toddler, has grown into a bubbly, bright, and beautiful young lady. In college, she pursues her goals, as she does everything in life, with enthusiasm, determination, and love.

God holds a special place for this child. The words "sharing and caring" are written all over her. She just naturally seems to put the needs of others first. While another first child might whine from the weight of it all, Chrissy eagerly takes on the responsibility and trust — willingly serving as confidante, cheerleader, and stand-in mother whenever I am away. Her younger brothers and sisters look up to her in so many ways, yet she never seems to tire of offering them an abundance of encouragement, support, and strength. With Chrissy as our first child, it's no wonder we wanted another.

Which brings us to Tim.

Tim was born to us on July 7, 1970. He saw life as an invitation to mischief, adventure, and amusement. Here was the child that taught me how to relax and enjoy life. He also helped straighten out my priorities. Until Tim came on the scene, my home and my schedule ran like clockwork. I was nearing perfection, but God took care of that bad habit with the gift of one energetic two-year-old. He was into EVERYTHING, bending every rigid parenting rule I had set. With Tim, I learned that a spotless home or end tables crowded with sentimental knickknacks was far less valuable than a happy household.

Today, Tim stands an easy six feet. He still tackles life the way he tackled knickknacks, bike-riding, skateboarding, and waterskiing — with gusto bordering on heart failure (mine — not his). He's a "car man" who loves tinkering with old jalopies when he's not busy with college, his part-time job at a gas station, or the sweet young thing he finds far more captivating than classrooms, college, or cars.

Known for his tender heart and quiet ways, Tim today

12

is considerate, helpful, hardworking, and fun to have around. He brings to mind the old adage, "Still waters run deep."

If there's anything I've learned as a mom to many, it is that each child is an entirely unique personality. Never mind if they resemble in looks or mannerisms the style or features of another. Each one is incredibly different. I think God engineers this phenomenon in order to keep things lively. Our third child made that lively difference.

I can still remember that early morning (5:00 A.M.), December car ride home from the airport with our frightened, little, almond-eyed, eighteen-month-old Filipino daughter in my arms. Johnny could hardly take his eyes off of her as he grasped the steering wheel with one hand and patted her reassuringly with the other. In spite of her sparse hair, and the questionable medical problem previously diagnosed as a cephal hematoma on the head, she was gorgeous and we were in love!

"Boy, I can't believe we're so lucky," Johnny kept saying as we drove across town to our home with our sleeping Tina Marie.

"I thought we were supposed to be doing something for her, but I think SHE'S the one who is doing something for us." So she did.

This first adoption was not without trial, however. Having lived in an orphanage for fifteen months and a foster home for three months, she was not about to let herself feel secure with us, the third change in her young and mobile existence. Biting and throwing food were her special ways to get even. For weeks she would scream if the other kids even touched me, even though she herself would demonstrate little in the way of hugs or affection. It took months — no years — and the change was gradual, yet gratifying.

In spite of the shaky start, we learned through Tina, how easy it was to open our hearts to a child not "flesh of our flesh," nor "bone of our bone."

The most wonderful thing about Tina has been watching our "Rosebud" blossom into a prize-winning American Beauty. She is now outgoing, athletic, and fun-loving. An over-achiever, she prods herself to be the best she can be, both at academics and in sports. At home, she is my right-arm kitchen aide and cook. Best of all, she is warm, affectionate, and genuine. How incomplete our lives would be without Tina.

Tony, whom we instantly tagged our Vietnamese "miracle baby," arrived on December 21, 1972 — five days after Tina's arrival. He came thanks to a government-issued Emergency Medical Visa, which probably saved his frail, young life. His needs were urgent. He was two months old and weighed a scant five pounds, suffering from malnourishment, starvation diarrhea, and severe dehydration. In addition, we were warned of "possible deafness and suspected retardation."

The old saying, "Be careful what you pray for — you might get it," applies here. We had been so eager to adopt. After waiting over a year for Tina, and having her visa and travel constantly delayed with warnings she may never come at all, we applied for a baby from Vietnam. We never dreamed the two would arrive within days of each other.

Christmastime 1972 is one holiday we'll long remember. We had gone from two to four kids, all under the age of four-and a half, with three in diapers. Our two new arrivals had their days and nights mixed up so they were wide-eyed and ready while we were craving sleep. Besides the serious medical conditions of the new arrivals, John and I came down with the Asian flu and were sicker than we had ever been in our lives. Looking back, those first weeks were little more than a blur of crying, around-the-clock feedings, trips to the doctor, and "adjustments."

What a beginning! Shaky and slow, to say the least, but we found good medical care and supplemented it with twenty-four-hour love.

After that, I walked round the house with Tony strapped to me like a papoose so that he would feel the security and holding he desperately needed. Within months

14

he was thriving. We're convinced that prayer and twenty-four-hour attention produced the results — a carefree, six-teen-year-old track and wrestling team enthusiast, who has never heard of the word "limitation."

Tony is our "spark" and quick wit, and enjoys every-thing but schoolwork, responsibility, and routine. For all his electric energy, and "cool" manner, there's an underly-ing faith and solid goodness in Tony that always shines through. Academics may not be Tony's forte, but we're bet-ting already that whatever he does, his genius will be felt and respected by many. I'm praying I'll be around to nod and say, "I knew you could do it, kid."

It's not that we weren't grateful for this little family. We certainly saw in each son and daughter the specialness of God's creative hand. Yet it took a Marriage Encounter weekend in 1974 for us to realize that we had failed to con-sult our Heavenly Father about our decision to have no more children.

"Do you think you have all the children God intends you to have?" was the question posed to John and I that weekend. Our answer set us on a course which opened our hearts, widened our horizons, and changed our lives. Until then, we had contentedly believed we had reached our peak. The retreat helped us believe God had something more in store.

We returned home and called an adoption agency.

Within months, we were busy hanging wallpaper, paint-ing bedrooms, and repairing second-hand bunkbeds and dressers for the arrival of Vo Dinh Thanh, whom we would call Daniel Thanh. The information we had on our soon-to-be-son was sketchy at best. He was six, seven, or eight; had lived his entire life in the polio wing of a Saigon, South Viet-nam hospital; walked with a limp as a result of polio; and, according to the nurses, was "a happy, self-sufficient little boy."

We sent him letters, cards, pictures, and clothing to help him prepare for us. The snapshot we received in return revealed a handsome lad standing tall under a tree.

15

His arms were at his side and his shorts exposed one leg slightly smaller than the other, with his little socks curling down around the shoes. It was Daniel's whimsical smile, however, that heightened our eagerness for his coming.

It was now 1975 and Daniel's arrival plans were set and canceled several times because of the waging war and the turmoil in Saigon. The inevitable "fall of Saigon" to communism threatened him and hundreds of other orphans who were awaiting new homes and families. We felt so helpless, even our prayers seemed lacking.

On April 4, 1975 (Good Friday morning) news came over the air waves that an Air Force C5A transport plane carrying 243 orphans had crashed in a nearby rice field outside of Saigon. Somehow we knew our Daniel Thanh was on that flight. It took two agonizing days before official notice was sent to waiting families. We were one of them. Our son had been killed as he lay strapped to the floor of that cargo plane, the seats having been removed to airlift out as many children as possible. There are absolutely no words to describe our anguish and sorrow. In our minds and in our hearts, Daniel was our son.

As John and I held each other that April morning and sobbed, he uttered what we both wondered, "How could this be part of God's plan? . . . Maybe we weren't meant to have another child."

We resolved to wait and trust. We had been so certain God was calling us to be open to a youngster with a special need.

A month to the day that Daniel died, we received word that a little five-and-one-half-year-old, racially-mixed Cambodian boy (the same age as our Tim) needed a family. He spoke no English and was recovering from minor medical problems. There was no doubt what we would do.

Our household was joyful for the first time in a month. Timmy, almost five, was the most excited of all. He was going to have a new brother his "very own size."

The homecoming and adoption of our son, whom we named Charlie, was far more wonderful than we ever dreamed possible. From Charlie, we learned to bridge language, racial, and cultural barriers with love.

Charlie was our first black-skinned child and Johnny and I still laughingly recall that first night home when we undressed him and washed his dark chocolate-in-color frame in our white porcelain tub.

"This one may take some time getting used to, dad," I quipped to John as he looked on. Within twenty-four hours, our Charlie, though unable to speak English, had already begun to carve a niche in our hearts. He was our son.

A frightened, nightmare-tormented child who had witnessed death as an everyday occurrence, grew before our eyes in his ability to trust, accept, and love. We grew right along with him.

Tim and Charlie became inseparable — looking like the wonderful "salt and pepper" combination our "melting pot" family had become. Tim was tall, blonde, quiet, and shy. Charlie was short, dark, gregarious, and outgoing. Charlie, who spent his first American school years catching up to his peers, graduated from high school alongside of Tim. He graduated with National Honor Society recognition.

Looking now at this college-bound son, I could not love him more had he been born to us. If his Cambodian mother were alive and could see him now, she would beam with pride. What a fine job she had done those first five crucial years. What a privilege for me to be the "second mother" in Charlie's life.

I must say here that prejudice by family and friends is an issue that faces many couples who adopt children of other races. It did ours, and when it happened, there was anger, hurt, frustration, and tears. **Prayer** and **time** were the only things that scaled the walls of opposition.

The addition of Theresa a black/Caucasian, two-and-one-half-year-old toddler, brought our total to six children under nine years of age. Theresa was diagnosed with serious medical and mental limitations and required a little more tender loving care. She brought to us a special kind of challenge — the unknown. To us, she was perfect. She needed us, and we needed her.

Today, Theresa is a confident, kind, and fun-loving teen. School doesn't come easy for Theresa, but she is a hard worker and is holding her own beautifully. Her real talent lies in her musical ear. She loves music and has a voice like one of God's most melodious angels. If academics were put to lyrics, Theresa would be a genius.

Certainly now, we thought, our family was complete. Our hands and house were full. Neighbors used to ask, "Just where are you going to put them all?"

Our little three-bedroom rambler was crammed to the corners with three kids to a bedroom. The closets were bursting; boxes were stored under beds and our kitchen was so tiny that folding chairs replaced a once-matching settee.

We began to pray for larger quarters. Two years later, our prayer perseverance brought us a home twice the size of our first. In fact, our mortgage was so affordable and our bedrooms so numerous that while signing the escrow papers, I said to my husband jokingly, "You know the Bible verse that from those that are given more, more will be required? I sure hope this isn't some kind of a sign!"

It didn't take us long to find out. One month after our move I had "gotten myself pregnant" (as John likes to jokingly tell it). It had been nine years since I had given birth (Timmy being our last "home grown") and I was apprehensive.

Actually, I was downright miserable. Why? You would think after having six kids already that one more would make little difference. But it did to this Mom. I was looking forward to Theresa going to kindergarten in the fall and being able to do something I wanted to do. After all, I reasoned, I'd surely done my bit for God and country. I was hoping to join a crusade, start a cause, or just sit home and study the gum under my kitchen table.

Thankfully, God was at the controls and our beautiful, dimpled darling Mary Elizabeth was born on St. Patrick's

Day (March 17), 1978. This one was destined to become the "pet" of the entire family.

Mary Elizabeth's birth taught us once again to trust the Lord. She seemed to have been born with a perpetual smile and she thrived on the noise, attention, and ever-present love that we and her older brothers and sisters showered upon her.

Today, Mary, a pre-teen, is affectionately nicknamed the "Sponge" and is the eyes and ears of the family as she absorbs the latest gossip and happenings. Known for her casual ("relaxed") lifestyle, she seems to collect clutter and debris for a hobby, leaving a trail wherever she goes — papers, books, shoes, socks, brushes clothes, library books, you name it. I have threatened to superglue them to her person and her roommates (Tina and Chrissy) constantly threaten eviction, but no one can stay mad at "little Mary" for long. She's just too darn sweet-natured and lovable.

All of us were so delighted with Mary's birth, we just knew she had to have a companion close in age. This time it was we who surprised God — as we begged for more.

Eighteen months later, God heard our "pleas" and sent us (via Mom's tummy) Angela Marie — another of His creative "differences." She was captivating as an angel, and as angelic as Dennis the Menace.

Angela today is the social gadfly of the younger set. She is nicknamed "May I" by her adoring Dad because she's always asking to visit a friend, go to a party, have a party, or call someone on the phone. She just began her first year of piano lessons and eagerly awaits her stage debut. To Angie all the world is indeed a stage and her daily performances keep us all in stitches. Angie will make our growing old fun as we stand by and watch her unfold.

Valentine's Day, 1981, brought us another "import." Vincent (estimated to be about nine or ten) arrived from Calcutta, India. He had some serious physical handicaps, including a cleft palate, hearing loss in both ears (requiring aids) and cerebral palsy in his legs. His greatest obstacle, however, was emotional. He was a child who had suffered a lifetime of neglect, abuse, and abandonment. We heartbreakingly learned that he could not accept the "smothering, stifling, commitment" of family life.

With Vincent, we learned the real meaning of unconditional love, and the most difficult lesson of all — that some handicaps simply cannot be overcome once a youngster's childhood has been filled with hurt and hostility. After a five-year struggle, involving hospitalizations, treatment centers, and on-going psychological therapy, he (at age sixteen) chose to live in a supervised foster arrangement. We keep in touch. Yet his loss was like a death in the family.

Kari Ann (another "tummy project") joined the chorus in 1982. She had a few setbacks with yellow jaundice and clubbed feet requiring casts. She first seemed to be a wee shadow of her sisters Chrissy, Mary, and Angela. But she has turned into a strong, self-assured little lass. Kari loves to chatter and is a constant smiler, hugger, and lover. She may resemble her sisters in appearance, but her pixie-ish charm is all her own. *Vive la joie!*

When Michael Joseph arrived via his mom on the Ides of March, 1984, his brothers and dad were so thrilled they hung an eight-foot banner heralding the news in front of our house.

Michael's manner and style is unusually thoughtful, reserved, and shy. He is a peaceful little gentleman, happiest when he's following his daddy around the yard, playing with his "little guys" or "snitching food" as mom cooks in the kitchen. His was another new personality and a stable force compared to the next child.

Just as things were becoming routine, whatever that is, Eve Furseth, the adoption social worker who had lovingly entrusted most of the adopted little souls in our care, called to tell of us about a little newborn Mexican/American boy whose mother wished him to be placed in foster care, with the intention that he be adopted by a "large Catholic family." We were elated to be chosen. And Dominic Francis, our Spanish star, joined our constellation in October, 1985, bringing our total to twelve.

Dominic, whom we lovingly refer to as our "Mexican tornado," can turn things upside down faster than any kid I've seen. He is a bolt of lightening. The doctors would call him hyperactive, and he is, but he's also a loving, little four-year-old underneath the electrical wiring. His round, soulful, deep brown eyes and impish smile are oftentimes the only things that save him from the straight-jacket I'd like to wrap him in.

In May of 1987, John and I experienced perhaps the greatest challenge of our married lives. John was found to have a tumor on his brain. Located on the pituitary gland, it rested over the optic nerves at the base of the forehead. Surgery was swift and successful, thanks to the skilled hands of Dr. Harry Rogers, an experienced neurosurgeon. More importantly, we believe it was our family, friends, and surrounding community who literally lifted us up in prayer. The tumor was benign.

The neurosurgeon, internist, and endocrinologists prepared us for other side effects, however, including infertility because of the damage done to the hormonal system. Being over forty, and having twelve children already, this consequence did not worry us nearly as much as cancer, on-going health problems, or, worse of all — death. Our sole attention was preoccupied with praying for John's life and return to health. Imagine our surprise then, when I "got myself pregnant" again the following November.

Along came our caboose, Joseph Harold, who was born on July 13, 1988. Another of God's generous miracles. He's a carbon copy of many of the other "tummy" kids, and yet he's already demonstrating a personality and charm all his own.

Today, we have one young adult, six teenagers, four in grade school, and two pre-schoolers.

No matter how tight our budget has been there has always been somebody to help. We have received unexpected raises, a gift from a dying uncle and a thoughtful present from a neighbor. We've learned to live on faith, and in the process, we've seen that God is NEVER outdone in generosity. Any sacrifices on our part have been more than compensated for in other ways.

Still, I would be lying if I painted a completely happy-ever-after picture. We have had more than our share of sorrows, losses, and tears — perhaps more than a small family can ever imagine.

Just our sheer number, diversity of backgrounds, and personalities, emotional scars and adjustments, could keep a team of Mayo Clinic psychologists busy for months. There's been more failure and heartache than we ever thought possible. Yet the laughter, joy, and love more than offsets the days when I've felt frustrated, blue, or vowing that if I never saw another messy diaper, tantrummed kid, rebellious teen, or run-over toilet, I'd blink not an eyelid.

As we enlarged our family, and especially as we added our adopted children and worked through the emotional and physical challenges that accompanied their arrival, a strange and beautiful thing was occurring. Our faith and love was increasing. Were we doing something for these children? No. It truly was THEY who were doing something for us.

Whether by "tummy" or by adoption, we saw each child as a blessing and a uniquely different personality which only enriched what we already had. We began to understand in a personal way, the old adage, "Love never divides, it can only multiply."

The question, "Do you think you have all the children God intends for you to have?," made us realize that God wants to be included in every facet of our lives, and in our case He had something more in store.

Parenting a large family is not for everyone, but for us the "calling" — though sometimes seeming to be faint — has enriched us in a way that no cruise, Cadillac, or castle ever could.

# Chapter 2

# Wombs with a Window

Having just delivered Number 13, my seventh "home grown," I easily ignored the hospital invitation to attend the parents class down the hall. I could live without a "Welcome New Baby" course. Capturing an uninterrupted nap, curling up with a good book, or just staring at a wall free of handprints, magic marker or someone's sticky remains, was about all the motivation I wanted.

"I think this is one class even you might find interesting," my assigned nurse sweetly suggested as she pulled the thermometer from my mouth and unwound the blood pressure wrap. Curiosity always being my weakness, I marched down the hall.

Fascinating it was, and learn something I did!

Standing amidst a roomful of newborn babies and doting parents, was a child development specialist who moved from infant to infant, picking each one up as she went along while simultaneously explaining the importance of closeness, touch, and a baby's need for a sense of security.

She quietly and calmly talked to the infants, all the while demonstrating each one's skill at grabbing, holding, hearing, and seeing. Coming from an era when the "Old Wives' Tale" insisted that newborns were virtually unresponsive and "**only** saw shadows the first six weeks of life," it was fun to watch even the fussiest and most uncooperative of her subjects, melt, mellow, and dutifully perform in her reassuring arms.

One little guy followed a colorful toy with his eyes. In fact, not just his eyes, but his entire head moved from side to side, as he attempted to catch the object with his hours-old stare. A baby girl tracked the sound of a shaking rattle; and a robust little nine pounder did a simulated "moon walk" for his absorbed audience.

When the instructor came to our seven-hour-old, Joseph, he was crying and fussing. Ignoring his frustration she scooped him from his isolet and began to softly speak into his face. His near instantaneous calmness and tranquil demeanor at her wooing was example enough of the importance of tenderness and holding.

"Newborns," she said, "recognize and will react to gentle reassuring voices and the sounds they were used to hearing BEFORE birth. In fact, in most cases, they've already formed attachments. Not just to mom but to other family members and loved ones."

"Aw, come on now. Isn't that stretching it just a bit?" I thought to myself. It stands to reason that a newborn will recognize his mother's voice as the one he has listened to in utero for the past nine months — but to recognize the voices of others?

She must have read my mind.

Proving her point, she placed our hefty little six-pound prince between her and my husband, inviting him to compete by talking to Joseph at the same time that she did. Up to that point Joseph appeared totally captive to her charm. Within seconds of hearing dad's baritone-yet-tender words, Joseph's head whipped a full 180 degrees, to dad's direction — and there it remained. Eyes fixed on dad.

Just then, our oldest daughter, Chrissy, came into the room. She had not seen her newborn brother and was hoping to steal a glimpse before the rest of the pack, like a herd of locust on their prey, descended "en mass," for the afternoon visitors session. Again, the child specialist suggested the test and — you guessed it — the moment Chrissy began to croon Joseph's name, his head turned from the attention-getting instructor to his oldest big sister. And so too, did he virtually lock his gaze in her direction. No amount of gentle coaxing, cooing or wooing could snatch his devotion. He knew this voice was familiar and a real love.

When it was my turn and Joseph's pink body, clad only in a T-shirt and diaper, jerked around with such obvious recognition and devotion, my eyes revealed what my heart could not hold. I cried.

Since then, I have learned even more about what sophisticated, complex, and developed little miracles babies really are — even before birth.

Recently, investigators at the University of Southern California (USC), through the insertion of a special microphone in the uterus, discovered that almost every external sound — some as distant as twelve feet away — can be heard by the pre-born child in the womb.

With a household of five teens, one young adult, and six kids under ten, I can't imagine the excitement our Joseph consumed over the nine months before he was born.

Scientists in Queens University in Belfast, Northern Ireland, made an equally fascinating discovery. They found that newborn babies actually can recognize the signature tunes of television soap operas that they heard while still in the womb. In an experiment the infants who were exposed to a popular TV soap opera before birth, immediately stopped crying and "became alert, as if they were watching the show" when the program's theme song was played.

One researcher suggested the babies associated the music with relaxation because their mothers were calm and attentive when watching the program.

Dr. Marshal Klaus, chairman of the Department of Pediatrics, Michigan State University, and Phylis Klaus, psychotherapist, who hold symposiums on "The Care of The Newborn and Its Family," contend that the senses of taste, smell and touch are highly developed by birth. Variations in temperature, texture, moisture, pain and pressure are also discriminated by newborns.

Dr. Norm Virnig, who is Director of Neonatology at St. Cloud Hospital, and a Clinical Associate Professor of Pediatric and Family Practice at the University of Minnesota, says, "A pregnant mother most certainly can transmit love and a sense of well being to her preborn child." So too, he says, "does a baby in the womb sense the mother's anxiety, irritation, and stress. The baby shows this by moving around more and by bouts of restlessness."

No wonder the Chinese for centuries counted a baby's time in utero as the "first year" of life. Even without sophisticated equipment or technological know-how, they sensed the intricate, yet fragile, development of a child before birth.

Obviously we are only just beginning to comprehend what effects the outside world has on an infant in the womb.

With Joseph we learned that he knew far more about us than we had even begun to discover about him. In fact, he had a full nine-month jump on us. He had a womb with a window.

We may never fully know everything about babies before birth, but perhaps we're beginning to realize the most important fact of all: When pregnant mothers and their inborn get tender loving care and support their window to the world is full of promise and inviting hope.

to Mom. From Charlie.

*Chapter 3*

# The Baby Barometer

Quite frankly, neither John nor I dreamed that the vows we spoke on that beautiful, sun-filled day in May (1966) would alter the course of our lives so drastically.

At that time we thought maybe four children would be great. But God had other ideas, as He nudged our heartstrings to make way for our seven "home-growns" and six "imports." I shudder to think what we would have missed had we not been open to God's call.

I used to believe that love had its limits, and that couples who parented many (i.e., more than six) were hardly more than Brownie leaders or group-home caretakers, with little "quality" time (whatever that means) available for individual affection or attention. Surely, parents of a large family exhausted every ounce of energy they owned just RAISING their brood.

How wrong I was.

I came to realize, as each one arrived, that our love — for each other and for our children — grew *in spite* of the increased workload, worries, and wakeful nights and more importantly *because* of our willingness to welcome one of God's little ones into our lives. I learned too that love never divides, it always MULTIPLIES.

I'll admit there were times when I wanted more children and the powers that be, i.e., finances, agency red tape, inter-country snags, immigration roadblocks or "hesitant" husband, stood in the way. Those were the times I turned to my spiritual allies; the Blessed Mother and St. Therese of Lisieux (the "Little Flower"). To St. Therese I would say a novena (a series of prayers said each day for a number of consecutive days).

Maybe St. Therese listened because she was so young

when she died, or perhaps because of her own childlike heart. All I know is that the dreams and hopes that seemed impossible, became reality after I sought the Blessed Mother and St. Therese's prayerful intervention on behalf of our family-planning goals.

All in all, the Baby Barometer we used in deciding whether or not to add another, went something like this:

\* **Prayer.** It is the most vital ingredient in a Christian marriage. Through the years, and especially with regard to having children, we've learned to rely on God, the Third Partner in our Marriage. After all, He knows far better than we what is best for our lives.

\* **God does provide.** "Close your eyes, trust, and watch the miracles unfold," has proven true in more instances than I care to admit. Again we learned through our own tremblingly weak acquiescence that when we prayerfully cooperate with the Lord, HE PROVIDES the resources needed (be it financial, emotional, or physical).

\* **Unity of spouses.** Both of us must be in agreement. There have been times when only one of us felt a readiness or openness to add another child. One isn't a majority. When there isn't total agreement, especially with such a lifetime decision that affects the entire family, God does not want one partner running ahead of the other.

Speaking personally, "restraint" is not my most outstanding quality. I confess. I've been known to say a Novena to St. Therese (the "Little Flower") on occasion, when my heart told me "there's room for one more" and Johns' was saying "enough — enough."

Yes, there were times when John and I were not in harmony. I am the impulsive, impetuous, instinctive person. If my heart and I agree, I'm inclined to act now and think later. Thankfully, John, is the "weigher," the rational, logician who considers all the possibilities in decision making. The compromising result has been a "Let's wait and pray" resolve. After all, if God wants a couple to have another baby, He'll do the heart changing. And He did.

**\* Financial, physical, emotional, spiritual security.** The question might boil down to: Can we afford another child right now? Will it put a strain on either our physical or emotional well being? Are we both ready? (Is anyone ever really ready?)

When we talk about "afford," I'm not talking about providing a room for each kid, a college-paid education, and the ability to plan for every fork in the road. I don't think God really wants us to have such control over every facet of our lives and futures. I'm talking about living comfortably without being stretched to the limits.

God does not want any of His children overburdened or on the verge of collapse. Thus questions of financial security, physical health, emotional well being, and marital stability must all be considered. If this is prayerfully done the spiritual question takes care of itself.

Not every married couple is meant to parent thirteen kids. On the other hand, it's hard to imagine God telling the majority of Americans (who want for little) to "stop at two."

**\* We're in it together.** One of the reasons we enjoy being parents to so many kids is because we never saw it as a "his" and "hers" endeavor. We both pitch in when and where we can and both believe in sharing the tasks.

Sad to say, many a woman would be only too willing to go through another uncomfortable labor, delivery, and mound of dirty diapers if only her husband would help lighten her load when he's home, instead of adding to the weight of it. So, too, are there husbands who feel stretched beyond bounds by a martyred wife who "saves" for him all the most unpleasant jobs, or runs up exorbitant expenses.

Marriage is not a "fifty-fifty" proposition. Really it's a one hundred-percent proposal, with each spouse giving one hundred percent to the other.

**\* What does God ask of us?** Our Christian faith tells us that children are a gift from God. "Do you think you have all the children GOD intends for you to have?" was a question posed to us on a Marriage Encounter weekend that challenged us for the first time to include Our Heavenly Father in our family-planning decisions.

In particular, Pope Paul VI's encyclical, *Humane Vitae*, instructs married couples to be *open* to the possibility of new life unless there is grave reason to postpone or avoid pregnancy. The Catholic Faith views children as a blessing.

In our own lives, we came to realize that if we truly intended to deepen our faith life, we could not shut God out. We needed to be open to His Will in all areas of our life. Thus, saying, "No," to even the possibility of children, was essentially saying no to God Himself, the Creator of all life.

Some couples will be blessed with many children and will endure the up and down bittersweet blessings that follow. For others, a life of infertility may grant them relative leisure and freedom, and yet the burden of wanting children is so heartrending, their only consolation maybe their faith, and a relinquishment to God's will.

In all situations, an openness, a surrender, to Our Heavenly Father is the surest avenue to marital happiness.

Lack of unity on the crucial issue of having children, could become the center of much disharmony or dissension in a marriage. Many Christian spouses have had to bow to the will of reluctant mates, thus denying their own desire for more children. Patience and persistent prayer will do far more to heal this open sore than arguing, pleading, and nagging. It is far better to make a reasoned case letting your wishes for another child be known to your spouse, and then release it to God.

* **Priorities.** Bombarded by a "Me-first" secular society, too many couples today allow their priorities to be placed in an upside-down order. You can always take that trip, have a career, go back to school, or climb the ladder to success. But, you can't always have a baby. Don't let selfishness, greed, feminist dictates, or fear ruin the only opportunity you may have.

Needless to say, some priorities cannot be ignored. Others can be postponed and rearranged. And then there are those you find, after an honest assessment, that should be abandoned altogether.

31

For all the faults and shortcomings of the old "Rhythm Method" of family planning, perhaps its greatest asset was its uncertainty and unreliability. Many a Catholic couple who, bowing in obedience to God's plan, saw their rhythm surprise babies as the greatest blessings of all.

Ah, what a few healthy little "surprises" in this day and age of planned and perfect pregnancies might do for all of us!

**\* Don't be influenced by those around you.** Do what you and your hearts know to be God's will for YOU.

A friend called the other day to tell me about her married daughter's new and lavish home. "She has a home most women dream of having. The kind you see in the decorator magazines with everything coordinated and matched. The furniture is new. No nicks, no handprints, and nothing out of place. Of course, they have no children, you know," lamented my friend, who confessed to wishing they had just come instead from visiting a house far less elegant, yet inhabited by a grandchild or two.

What convincing consolation could I conjure up, after mopping up from the twenty-four-hour flu and hearing from a thoughtful neighbor that Michael (age five), Dominic (age four), and Joseph (age one) had just been exposed to chicken pox.

No nicks, no handprints, nothing out of place. I can't imagine it. But then, I also can't imagine the emptiness and void there would be if there were no Chrissy, Tim, Charlie, Tina, Vincent, Tony, Daniel, Theresa, Mary Elizabeth, Angela, Kari, Michael, Dominic, or Joseph. I guess I'll stick to handprints, flu, and chicken pox.

I can't hug a polished table.

# Chapter 4

# Pregnant Again?

Most pregnant women could fill a book with remarks others make about their condition.

While it was once considered brash and offensive to interrogate pregnant women, expectant mothers today are routinely probed with inquiries, insinuations and opinions. The only surprise is the victim's ability to remain composed, tolerant, and perhaps even cordial during the inquisition.

"How can you afford it?" and "Does John make that kind of money?" are perhaps far kinder than "Not again!" or "Are you sure you know what you're doing?"

Is any parent ever REALLY sure?

I have encountered those who bluntly inquire, "Weren't you using anything?" If I answer at all, I usually respond, "No. Were we supposed to?" Others ask if it was "wanted." I quickly assure such people that ALL of our children were wanted and loved.

If I could start a national campaign for anything, it would be to abolish the term "unwanted child." What a disgraceful label to hang on a defenseless baby — whatever the circumstances that surround his or her birth.

Carol, a friend of mine and first-time mother-to-be was told upon announcing her good news, "I didn't think you were that type."

She quickly, yet kindly, responded, "And what TYPE is that?"

Pregnant women are grilled — albeit gently — about many issues, including their capability ("Don't you have your hands full already?"), age ("But you're so young!" or conversely, "Oh, my dear, at your age?"), and other responsibilities. For the women over thirty, the most piercing question is, "Have you thought of how old you'll be when he or she finishes high school?" — as if senility sets in after fifty.

Others express concern about the strain another child may have on the existing family unit. "How did the kids take the news?" one woman asked my neighbor Pat, a young mother of three — sounding as if she were referring to a death in the family rather than to a new life.

Expectant parents with more than three children already may encounter, as we did, the phony compassionates who say, "Poor little Chrissy (the oldest). She shoulders such responsibility." Rather than viewing an addition as a welcome delight and playmate to the others, this comment conjures up images of an oldest child strapped to a household of dirty diapers, babysitting, and clinging baby brothers and sisters.

A recent magazine article agonized over whether to have a second child. It arrived too late in my own mailbox, but I wonder how many millions of first-time parents were affected negatively by the not-so-subtle, anti-too-many-children message.

It seems this anti-child mentality permeates all of society. Parenting is belittled by the media, radical feminists, and even some of our own family and friends. A kind of mind-set suggests that planning no children, or never more than two, should be our national goal.

There was a time, not so long ago, when a woman, "with child" encountered only well-wishers and supporters regarding her baby's upcoming arrival. Those who were pitied and prayed for were the couples who wanted to have children but couldn't. The minority who openly rejected parenthood were so outside the norm, that they were the ones who became the unfortunate object, in some circles, of inquiry, harassment, and unsolicited advice.

The tables have radically turned.

Along with the masculinization of womankind in the 60s and 70s, came the notion that children should no longer be viewed as a natural byproduct of love and marriage. Only the religiously inspired seem to consider children as a blessing and the "fruit" of married love. One need only attend a conventional wedding ceremony to realize that the word "children" is rarely mentioned (Catholic Church excluded), for fear of offending the betrothed.

Thankfully, the feminist campaign of chastisement toward mothers who choose child over career is passing. Yet, the decades of propaganda promulgated by the zero populationists, Planned Parenthood, and other abortion promoters have left their mark. A woman's economic, religious, marital, or age status matters not at all — someone out there sees her pregnancy as an invitation to snoop, to advise, or worse yet, to intimidate.

Surprisingly, many otherwise well-mannered people believe it perfectly appropriate to demand the most intimate details regarding a pregnancy and family life, while they would be incensed if asked to account for their own personal lifetime decisions. I wouldn't think of demanding someone explain the purchase of a $500,000 home, staggering accumulations of property, or extravagant living. Yet couples having children find themselves fair game to challengers.

Whether unwed and poor, or married and financially secure, many an expectant mother has been caught off guard by the curiosity of others.

Many critics accuse us of overpopulating. Articles have been written referring to couples with children as "breeders," putting us in the same category as rabbits and mice. Hostile as these remarks are, I feel they nonetheless deserve a sincere reply. Poverty, famine, and inadequate food distribution are definite problems in parts of the world. All caring Americans would do well to share our abundance with those who have such critical needs. But overpopulation in America? Empty classrooms, laid-off teachers, and recent statistics warn of a future crisis caused by an aging populace and a steady population decline as the U.S. continues to remain "below replacement level."

We may find ourselves like some of our European counterparts who offer family subsidies and cut-rate rents in an attempt to lure women into staying home and having a family. France is but one nation whose government offers fringe benefits to boost its sagging population.

Today's children will inherit a strained Social Security system, exploding health-care costs, and an unbelievable federal deficit. We adults will be turning to them for our medical needs, security, and protection. Rather than questioning their existence, I should think we would be welcoming their arrival. In fact, aren't children the greatest natural resource of America, its future?

When Pat, my young (thirty-ish) neighbor was carrying Child Number Four, she confided to me her astonishment at the questions put to her. "Was it planned?" was the one most frequently asked. And then the customary follow-up: "Now, is this it for you?" — suggesting that she should reveal her family-planning intentions to all inquirers — leaving nothing, of course, to nature, prayer, or (Heaven forbid) God.

Dorothy, another expectant friend experienced a different reaction when others learned there was a seventeen-year gap between the baby-to-come and its big sisters: "Oh! This must be a second marriage?" As if she and her husband, Mike, just couldn't be elated or eager to "start all over again" with this little "caboose."

"Not on your life," my friend Dorothy kindly retorted, "We're tickled, and so are our two teen-aged daughters."

Joyce tells of the time she was in labor with her fifth child and a "well meaning nurse asked me three times if I'd like to be scheduled for a tubal ligation." Quick on the comeback, Joyce responded, "No. But you could shoot the guy that got me into this."

Quite frankly, I am seldom bothered by inquisitors. As the mom-of-many, its probably presumed, by now, that I am past the point of either education, help, or shame. Whew!

I did earn my badge, however. There was the day when I was about eight months pregnant standing in a checkout line and a stranger walked up to me and said, "I'm sure glad it's you and NOT me."

I looked at her and with my most syrupy sweet smile said, "And so am I."

On another occasion, during my hospital stay after having given birth to our much awaited, Michael Joseph, a discharge nurse gave me a "family planning pamphlet," routinely given, I later learned, to all OB patients. The brochure described various methods of birth control, with the accompanying failure rates, and ultimately recommended "early abortion" if such contraceptive "failure" occurs, in order "to avoid late-stage complications."

Here I was with a beautiful new baby boy, and this institution of "healing" was advising me and other mothers like me (on a "routine" basis) on how to avoid having another baby. Obviously this facility was unaware of the decade-long "under population" problem (below "replacement level" according to the United States Census Bureau) this country is experiencing.

I waited until my stitches healed and my anger cooled and wrote the hospital administrator expressing my disappointment at the insulting, pro-abortion, and anti-child handout. His letter in response, I must admit, surprised me. He agreed that the material in question was indeed "offensive" and ordered it removed.

One wonders, however, how many other women over the years have been exposed to such propaganda, or how often this is done "routinely" at other hospitals around the country. I re-learned a major lesson in this exchange. The old adage, "Even one person can make a difference," is, indeed, true.

In my view, the negative remarks that cut most deeply into young parents are those made by the very people they had hoped would be their support system. A newly announced pregnancy might elicit admonitions of "Not again!" or "Don't tie yourself down anymore!" or "Have you thought of all the work this involves?" (As if we want to be reminded) — from even the closest of family and confidants. Years ago it was suggested by some that "God will provide." Some today may scorn such blind faith and yet I wonder if most parents would prefer that trusting tone to one that shrieks, "I hope you know what you're doing." It's little wonder parent support groups are springing up all over.

Perhaps, it's long past time for Christians to go on the offensive when the "pregnant-again" question is asked.

It's time we gently and lovingly remind the forgetful that all babies are created (with unique purpose) by our Divine Creator, and although the months of morning sickness, hormonal imbalance (which can cause an otherwise-eager woman to feel depression, fear, and sometimes even temporary rejection regarding her pregnancy) may cloud an apparent delight, we rest secure in the knowledge that God has promised the "best is yet to be."

*(Adapted from: National Catholic Twin Circle, Home Life Magazine, St. Anthony Messenger)*

# Chapter 5

# Modern Moms Don't Hide

I'm not exactly sure when it was that I put aside my false sense of modesty. It could have been the muggy August Sunday I watched my impatient baby cry through morning Mass. It might have been that dingy basement "ladies" room at the shopping mall, that got my goat. Or, perhaps it was the time I waited, squirming infant in arms, for what seemed like hours, in the checkout line of a busy discount store. All I know is something cracked and I decided that in the future, "Wait, I won't," when nature calls and baby wants to nurse.

"Just give him a bust in the face," my wonderful Polish and practical mother-in-law used to say. And so I do.

When I was a young first-time mom, I treated nursing as if it were an unnatural, almost unwholesome event. As such, I went to great pains so as not to be discovered by others. Many a time I sat it out in parked cars, empty church basements, women's lounges, darkened hallways, and even closets, in order not to exploit my wares. I've seen more restrooms, latrines, back rows and back rooms than a cavalcade of cleaning ladies. Never mind the functions I left early or skipped altogether because of baby's eating schedule.

Well endowed I'm not, and yet I was certain that any clue as to what it was I was doing with my baby, could be construed as flauntingly intimidating to others. What a prude!

With the birth of Mary Elizabeth, (our third, via "mom's tummy"), I changed. I realized that nursing, if done politely and prudently, can still maintain an air of privacy, modesty, and dignity. With a little practice, I became adept at quietly and discreetly securing baby to breast. No longer ostracized to the out-of-way, baby was content and I was calm.

The first thing I learned from this experience was that it can be done subtly enough so that passersby are completely unaware. Some, in fact, stop to see the baby or want to make small talk, such as, "How old?" and "Boy or girl?" or "Is this your first?" (I never dare tell them). Many don't even catch on to my nursing until I TELL them. Which brings me to the second thing I realized. Those bystanders who did become aware were very accepting. In essence, most people love to see a little baby. And ten times out of ten, they'd prefer a happy, quiet, contented one, to one screaming and searching for supper.

"Have you ever tried to climb a row of bleachers while breastfeeding?" my friend Janice laughingly asked one day, as we swapped nursing stories. "When you want to attend your kids' games at the school gym, you find yourself doing all sorts of crazy things."

I was never good at balancing bars and heights, I conceded, but I did survive an all-family vacation (no small feat with my crew) to Disney World by nursing Baby Joseph through every exhibit from Epcot Center to Sea World.

Many moms like my friend Janice have lost their shyness, yet still maintain their poise and pride.

Mary, a friend in her early thirties, was delighted with her new baby Michael. Her other two children were school-age and this was her first attempt at nursing. "I was breastfeeding Michael and then supplementing with bottled milk, thinking it would be easier and *less embarrassing* when we were out in public. What a mess. He was jittery and so was I."

The hassle stopped when Pat, an older and "been-through-it" mother approached Mary after a women's church meeting they were attending. "Mary, the more you nurse, the more milk you will have for Michael. If you keep giving him bottles, your own milk will decrease and you'll get frustrated and so will little Mike. It's easier and faster for the baby to take formula from a bottle, but convenience will NEVER compare with the comfort, satisfaction, and nourishment he'll get at your breast. Why don't you just go ahead and nurse that little guy. No one really notices or objects." And so she did, and within a week, both Mary and baby were calmer.

Support for the nursing mother was not always so. There were times in the not-too-distant past, especially after World War II and in the 50s and 60s, when bottle feeding was billed as the easiest, least restrictive, most convenient, and up-to-date method of mothering. Pity the poor person who dared suggest that a suckling child was just as modern or "progressive." Even physicians, who knew better, began yielding to the demands of women who chose bottle over breast, swallowing the commercial propaganda that there was little beneficial difference in the feeding method used.

The late Dr. Lawrence Richdorf, a well-known pediatrician, is one doctor who unrelentingly differed. He began the first milk bank at the University of Minnesota after World War II in order to care for the sick and/or dying babies arriving for operations or medical care. He became renowned for his program of soliciting nursing mothers to donate their "excess milk" which was frozen and later used as needed for the little ones coming for care. "So many times," Dr. Richdorf said, "it was breast milk, and ONLY that, which was suitable to feed a sick or malnourished infant, especially those coming from foreign lands."

I was indeed fortunate to begin my days of mothering with this man as my pediatrician, who served more as my coach, cheerleader, and confidant.

Today we know breast milk offers a host of vitamins and nutrition to an infant far superior (unless a mother is malnourished or gravely ill) than any bottled commercial milk. In addition, a psychological bond is created between mother and child which, though intangible, forms a foundation for love that will unite them the rest of their lives.

Indeed, cows, horses, dogs, sheep, and other animals

perform the same function in order to feed their young. It is ONLY in the human species, however, that mother and young can look on and gaze at each other during the time of suckling. And rightly so, as it is ONLY in humans that such a gaze, when performed lovingly, can transmit a sense of security and love to a tiny infant like no other parenting act.

My girlfriend Nancy bottle-fed her first four children, never considering the advantages of breastfeeding until she was coaxed into "just trying it." Nancy did and was hooked.

"Why didn't anyone tell me?" she said. "Nursing is not only easier (no bottles, formula mixing, packing a day's supply for an outing, or walking on a cold kitchen floor to the refrigerator at 3:00 A.M.), it's also inexpensive and you have all the equipment you need right on you."

"But the REAL benefit" she added, "was the wonderful closeness I feel toward this baby. I really regret not nursing my others."

Perhaps if the world saw more mommies snuggling their young in public we would be more mindful of the tenderness, affection, and love so vital to family life. This is an all but misplaced or forgotten reality in the frantic-paced lives we lead. More prominent today are the constant and compassionless statistics which reveal an ever-increasing number of children who are victims of abuse, abandonment, and abortion.

What backward times we live in. In today's topsy-turvy world, breasts are seen hanging out of evening dresses, workout suits, wedding dresses, and school dresses. Bosoms are used to sell everything from blouses to beer, Buicks to beauty tips, and breakfast cereal to business aids.

Why is it acceptable for women's breasts to be viewed as objects for seduction, sex, and sin, yet offensive when exposed for the God-given task for which they were created?

In bygone eras, in cultures we may regard today as rigid or puritanical, the concept of a nursing mother nurturing her young was considered natural and normal. Some of the greatest artists — Leonardo DaVinci, Renoir, Matisse, Michelangelo, Botticelli, Cassatt, and Rembrandt, to name but a few — reverently portrayed the beauty of breastfeeding mothers on canvas. This artistic concept is sadly lacking in today's world.

The "art" of perversion and porn seems to dominate this so-called enlightened age of liberation; depicting women's busts in every fashion but for what they were intended. And, in America — the bigger the better — for ogling, but not for breastfeeding, that is.

And, oh, the lengths to which some misguided souls will go. I remember the two overly "well endowed" young women I met in a Chicago dress shop fitting room. They were comparing notes on "size" and price with regard to their recent "silicone/implant surgery" — operations now proven to be potentially cancerous and dangerous. And for whose benefit are the alterations done?

Like most caring moms, I didn't deliberately intend to nurse in public, but when I considered the way women's bodies have been commercialized and compromised; or the millions of children who have been treated as burdens rather than blessings; and when I hear otherwise intelligent people suggest that babysitters, bottles, nursemaids or nannies can adequately replace the presence of a nurturing mother — I was determined to show no shame for the times when nature called and baby and I got together for lactose and love.

mom's baby

Nurse

Timothy

mom.

Nurse and mom

810

# Chapter Six

# Going Against The Norm

I must confess, parenting a large family was never a premeditated plan on my part. I mean, who would deliberately set out to mother thirteen children?

In my young and carefree years I was the girl who cherished her freedom and independence. Working as a legal secretary, I enjoyed a modest wardrobe, drove a baby blue convertible, had a life of relative leisure, and dreamed of the day I would set sail and "see the world." Little did I imagine then that I would end up married and viewing the world through the eyes of the seven kids born to my husband and me and the six racially-mixed kids we adopted, (four of whom came from foreign shores — about as close as I'll ever get to "seeing the world").

**Motherhood**
Let's be honest. It has its suicide moments. In fact, whether mom to one or to many, there are days when even the best of our ranks would eagerly trade places with a kamikaze pilot on a mission, rather than face another snarling teen, saucy seven-year-old, tantrummed and terrible toddler, colicky newborn — or the sheer boredom of doing the same monotonous chores done six times the day before.

Yes, there have been times when I've been tempted to quit; to join an animal rights group or just sit home and study the crayon marks on Dominic's bedroom wall, rather than go through another day of full-time mothering. But I'm willing to bet most everyone has had that "run-from-it-all" fantasy on occasion.

When I was a first-time mother, I used to wonder how far parental love could stretch. How naive I was! Shared love in a large family can best be described by the parable of the loaves and the fishes. The more passed around, the more there remains in the basket.

After twenty-plus years of parenting, my husband and I have discovered that love does not always conquer everything — but it sure helps!

It's hard to describe the added gifts that adoption brings to a family. We have all benefited so! When we first saw our eighteen-month-old Filipino throwing a temper tantrum as she spit at her brother and bit her new sister, I confess we may have wondered, "Will it work?" The thrill of her first accepting smile and loving kiss was all it took to know, "Of course, it will."

Adoption is a privilege when the bed wetting, nightmares, stealing, and testing stop and the trust begins. A privilege? No, it's a miracle! I cannot describe the joy at hearing our newly adopted Charlie (at age five) speak his first English sentence or write his name for the first time.

No one will ever know the feeling of being handed a five-pound, two-month-old baby boy diagnosed as "dying" from malnutrition, dehydration, and lack of stimulation, and then seeing that first family photo showing a chubby seven-pound bundle of love.

One of our sons came from war-torn Vietnam. At five years of age, he witnessed the loss of his whole family. Who can repair such hurt? We cannot, but God can.

Another son remembers a mother who abandoned him in the marketplace of India. After a series of jails, orphanages, hospitals, and street life, here he is. Who can heal those ten years of scarred memories? We cannot. But with God's help and prayer, we'll not give up believing anything is possible.

There seems to be an intangible quality in a large family that cannot be documented or adequately portrayed. Call it a camaraderie if you will, but a certain common union works to knit us together even under the stormiest conditions.

Oh yes, we have our problems, just as all families do. But through illness, death, teen years, racial prejudice, financial worries, attacks from the outside, or rebellion within, underlying is the knowledge that WE ARE FAMILY.

Next to the support for legalized abortion, perhaps one of the most shocking, if not repulsive, radical notions to come out of the feminist "liberation" movement is its wholesale rejection of the dignity and value of full-time motherhood. Even more appalling is the fact that this extremist element in American society, not only found a podium, but its dictates gradually became, first tolerant, then acceptable, and then the "norm."

Those of us who went against this "norm" in choosing to have children and to nurture them full-time as stay-at-home mothers, found ourselves head to head with not only radical, anti-faith feminists, but — quite disappointingly at times — some members of our own faith and family.

For a time, the country was even brainwashed to believe that couples must limit the number of their children (no more than two), because there was an over-population crisis. The results of such propaganda were: an avalanche of school closings, "Help Wanted" posters displayed in most store-front windows today, and "below replacement level" U.S. Census Bureau statistics which reveal the top-heavy crisis approaching, with more elderly than employed to support them.

How, and where, along the way, did America — traveling its "progressive" and liberated trail to the 90s — abandon its once universal belief that children were a "blessing" — a gift from God?

It's long past time that Christians band together in support of the unique role God bestows on married women, and to encourage those women, who, often at great personal and financial sacrifice, choose the career of full-time mother.

Perhaps I'm just prejudiced, but I'm one of those homebound "traditionalists" that some would call outdated, out of step, or just plain old-fashioned.

My equality, and millions of homemaking professional moms like me, will never be measured on whether or not we can lift that fire hose, tote that barge, or achieve a corporate position, but rather in the mere fact that as women, we and only we, can bear the gift of new life within our womb, and can nurture our young at the breast.

By choice, I am a full-time wife, homemaker and mother, and I readily concede that — excluding flu season, car-pooling a Blue Bird troupe, spring cleaning our boys' room, or enduring an outbreak of chicken pox — I love what I'm doing!

I admit, I would take in laundry, typing, other people's kids, or a bunch of baby barracudas, in order to stay home and care for my family. Sure, the work is tedious, uncreative, unfulfilling, downright boring, and financially unrewarding if measured by radical feminist standards, but not by my yardstick. It's the most meaningful, creative, adventuresome, fulfilling, and rewarding thing this woman can do. I'm helping to shape the future.

Because of popular folklore, a tragic stereotype has gone virtually unchallenged regarding the stay-at-home mother. Sadder still is the fact that much of the discrimination leveled at this chosen profession has come, not from chauvinistic, unenlightened men, but from the very persons we thought would stand in our defense — "liberated" women who champion what they consider more "meaningful" outside-of-home careers.

To set the record straight, full-time homemakers, like myself, who deliberately choose the career of homemaker, are not overweight, overindulged, under-educated, uninvolved, or uninformed. The majority of us are not hooked on TV soaps, game shows, or re-runs of Lawrence Welk. We don't sit around stuffing our faces with potato chips all day, mindlessly chatter for hours on the phone, or try to "create a new me" at diet farms, "the club," spa, bowling, or Bingo.

No. Our exercise, stimulation, and "ladder of success" is measured by the smiles, snuggles, hugs, and loves we give and receive from those we serve — our family.

This in no way is meant to slight the mom who MUST work outside the home in order to provide for her family. She deserves our support and prayers. The evidence remains, however, that the majority of full-time career mothers in today's work force are there not because of need, but because of greed.

Pope John Paul II, in his address to the United Nations (October 2, 1979) warned that "material goods by their very nature provoke conditionings and divisions; the struggle to obtain these goods becomes inevitable in the history of humanity. If we cultivate this one-sided subordination of man to material goods alone, we shall become incapable of overcoming this state of need."

He reminds us too that the desire for spiritual goods "does not divide people, but puts them into communication with each other." In his *Apostolic Exhortation on the Family* John Paul II insisted, "The Church can and should help modern society by tirelessly insisting that the work of women in the home be recognized and respected by all in its irreplaceable value."

The Holy Father challenges society to restore the superiority of the family and the individual over work. He suggests a "social re-evaluation of the mother's role, of the toil connected with it and of the need that children have for care." He also proposed that there be "grants to mothers devoting themselves exclusively to their families."

Don't ya love it? Career moms themselves, know from firsthand experience that no one — not a well-meaning relative, neighbor, friend, or manufactured kiddie care, can do for hire what we do for free. Whether it's an infant seeking the reassurance of a mother's arms, an adolescent in need of a tender touch, or a struggling teen looking for a listening ear, a mother's presence is vital.

After all, love builds like yeast. And love, like yeast, takes time, tenderness, aging, and care. It can't be scheduled, subsidized, or put on hold. Three cheers for the mom who makes the choice for her husband and her young, to be a full-time homemaker. Show me a full-time homemaker and I'll show you a woman of vision who is working to shape America's future — for generations to come.

# Chapter 7

# Making Big Christians
# Out Of Little Ones

"Parents are the first missionaries to their children," Father Frank often tells his Minneapolis parishioners. "If you succeed at nothing else in life, yet pass on the faith to your children, your lives will have been successful in God's eyes." A pretty tall order in today's world.

I'm sure most Christian parents have worried, as my husband and I have, about the influence of today's secular society and anguished as we have, over whether or not they've done a good job in forming a sound faith and value system in their young.

Pope John Paul II, in his *Apostolic Exhortation on the Family*, teaches that only by prayer can Christian parents "penetrate the innermost depths of their children's hearts and leave an impression that the future events in their lives will not be able to efface." In other words it all begins with us.

When my husband and I were new parents and our children were small, our faith was far less formed, far less secure compared to where we are today. We said our prayers before meals, never missed Sunday Mass, and occasionally went to confession, whether we needed it or not. Back then we considered ourselves "good Catholics."

As our little ones grew, we came to realize that our spiritual life was wishy-washy and shallow. We weren't as "good" as we thought we were. We could share most everything from sex to the stomach flu, but when it came to the spiritual or the idea of praying together outside of meals and church, the subject seemed "too personal" to approach. Having children actually gave the nudge my husband and I needed to get closer to God.

As new parents we realized quickly that children are born "parent-pleasers" and great imitators. If we wanted them to know and love the faith, we had to do more than assume they'd pick it up by osmosis. There could be no waiting until they were ready, or trusting they would learn it in religion class. That didn't mean we had to be perfect. What was important was that we be consistently faithful.

Speaking as a mom in the trenches, I would like to share a few ideas for young couples eager to pass on their faith:

* **Start young.** If your kids aren't used to going to church with you, praying **together** in the home, or observing religious practices, it's never too late to begin. But don't wait another day. Changing old ways becomes all the more difficult with each passing year, especially as children enter adolescence. These are the years that nature urges them to question and challenge many facets of their lives. If they didn't grow up with these practices, they are likely to rebel if all of a sudden you suggest saying the daily Rosary, reading and discussing a Scripture passage, or attending Mass together.

* **Attend Mass together as a family.** Unless sickness, a new baby, or conflicting schedules prevent otherwise, Mass is an occasion that should include the entire family. No matter how distracting this can be, there is a unifying bond created by worshiping together week after week.

If you have rambunctious pre-schoolers, don't give up, even if you must occasionally take them to the back of the church. In time, they will begin to imitate the reverence and silence they see in the people around them. It helps to sit toward the front where little ones can see more than just the backs of people's heads.

* **Make Sunday special.** With pressures coming at families six days a week, Sunday should be the one day we put away our office work, home chores, and unpleasant tasks. Planning something fun and relaxing for the whole family is a positive way to let your children know that Sun-

days are special because God made them special.

&ast; **Vary your mealtime prayers.** Praying together before meals is a good beginning. When youngsters are old enough, let them choose an additional prayer or reading. This will make the child feel a special part of family prayer and demonstrate the importance you place on thanking God.

A little parental guidance is needed here. One evening at mealtime, our daughter Chrissy asked if she could read a prayer from her religion book. As a first-grader, she read well but very S L O W. We naively consented and then sat for nearly ten minutes with our gravy and potatoes turning cold and dry, while she trudged through the Apostles' Creed. After that, we made up a selection sheet of short dinner-time prayers from which they could choose.

&ast; **Evening prayers.** When it comes to evening prayers, it is especially important to start young and not expect miracles. One mother tried to get her family to say the Rosary during Lent. Before this time they had never said more than a prayer before meals together. The family's resistance left her in tears and the others tense and defensive.

Another couple with teens ran into the same kind of difficulty. The father settled for saying one decade. This was agreeable to all but one stoic daughter who chose to stay in her room during prayer time. The parents persisted, ignoring the protester. Today this young lady is a committed Catholic mother of two children. Instilling Catholicism by osmosis does have its place!

In our own family, we found that even when it has been one of those hope-tomorrow-is-better days, there is a calming, soothing, and tenderly close experience that comes from kneeling together for nightly prayers.

As young parents we started with the Angel of God prayer. When we wanted to introduce the Rosary, we knew there would be resistance. We began by introducing the concept of one decade, gradually increased it to two decades, then three and eventually the entire Rosary. Today our little ones proudly take turns leading a decade.

"The Rosary takes twelve to fifteen minutes and is the most powerful weapon outside of the Mass that we have," my husband often reminds the kids.

In his *Apostolic Exhortation on the Family*, the Holy Father explains that Christian parents, "by reason of their dignity and mission" are called to educate their children in prayer. "Prayer," he says, "constitutes an essential part of Christian life" (*Covenant of Love*, Hogan, Richard and Le-Voir, John. Part III "The Role of the Christian Family" p. 204). What better example to a youngster than to see his father and mother kneeling in prayer.

**\* Persistence and patience.** Making big Christians out of little ones takes time, patience, and perseverance. Don't fall into the trap of giving up out of discouragement. Remember just WHO it is that doesn't want your family to get close to God. Remember, too, God promised His grace would be sufficient.

In marriages where the parents are of a different faith, or only one is actively Christian, the lack of interest, or worse — open disbelief — will have a trickle-down effect upon the children, who observe more than we think. The commitment of the Christian parent, however, also has a trickle-down effect and can be an overpowering force for good.

My friend, Annette, is a wonderful example. Annette's husband wanted no part of her Catholic faith. Or any other faith. He refused to attend any church or to even allow the display of a crucifix or holy pictures in the home. Annette prayed and patiently attended Church and religious functions alone. Gradually, over a five-year period, and with the arrival of their children, her husband began to attend Mass on holy days, and permitted the display of palms and a crucifix on the living room wall. As their children grew, Annette stepped up her prayer vigil in the form of a personal Novena to St. Joseph. Her vigilance paid off when her husband relented in his opposition and allowed the children to attend a Catholic elementary school. Today, it is Annette's husband, who talks with pride about the school's influence, and speaks about it being "well worth the financial sacrifice" to their blue collar and tight budget.

* **Make use of sacramentals.** The use of Holy Water, blessed candles, and palms can add much meaning to your children's faith and understanding. Michael, our enthusiastic four-year-old, imitated our every action at church. When we stood, he stood. When we genuflected, so did he. When we blessed ourselves with Holy Water, he too dipped his hand in the font. The imitation ended, however, when we saw him put his fingers immediately into his mouth — suck the dripping water from the ends of his fingers. To Michael, this ritual only made sense when done for the purpose of quenching thirst. Once we brought home our own bottle of Holy Water, hung up a font, and began the practice of blessing our children and each other, Michael learned to bless himself properly.

Lighting a vigil light at church and offering a special prayer for someone you know is another good example of visible faith. By your actions you are saying, "I believe prayer helps and I know God hears us."

* **Create Christian traditions and celebrations.** Your kids need to know that your faith is something to rejoice over and celebrate. Make a big deal every time a family member is baptized, confirmed, or receives First Holy Communion. We have established a tradition of celebrating with "Sacrament parties." We hope our children will long remember the special foods, baked goods, and visiting relatives and friends that made up our sacramental celebrations.

Create your own family traditions with special emphasis on the holy days, Advent, and Easter. One of our favorite Advent wreaths, made by our little ones using four candles and an egg carton shell with imitation grass around the edges is a simple, yet beautiful, way to draw our family together in prayer.

We also celebrate this season by becoming Advent Angels. We each draw the name of another family member and secretly pray for that person during Advent. We send little notes with surprises or do a household chore for the person whose name we have drawn.

Lent is another "faith-building time" to promote the value of "giving and giving up" for the love of God. Talk to your kids about what things you are giving up and let them know how difficult it is for you. We've found that most kids don't want to be outdone in commitment and endurance and eagerly rise to the challenge of penitential sacrifice.

This is also an opportune season to say the Stations of the Cross on Fridays or to take turns reading short Scripture passages.

Another Lenten denial at our house is to give up television except for news and special programs. Steeling ourselves against the initial complaints the first few years, we discovered a hidden reward — we spent more time in play with each other. The older kids took time to read to the younger ones, and all had more time to talk, listen, or play cards or board games with one another.

* **Encourage Christian reading.** A Catholic home should always have books available on the precepts of our faith and heroes the kids can look up to and imitate. The Bible, Catholic periodicals, and books on the lives of the Saints, and an up-to-date catechism is a good beginning. It should go without saying that there is no room in a Christian environment for lewd or pornographic material. Christ was quite clear about the sinfulness of those who cause scandal and confusion to children.

* **Actions speak louder than words.** It's not WHAT you say, but HOW you say it. If you appear faithful and consistent in your own faith, a far greater impact will be made, than all the tedious talk and teaching in the world.

One cardinal rule for Catholic parents is never to contradict the Church or complain about a priest or religious. Nothing is more spiritually harmful to an impressionable child who is so vulnerable to what a parent says.

Let your children see your need for prayer. Don't assume your children know your faith is important to you.

Show them. Something as simple as sharing a prayer intention — "Dad is so thankful today for his new job" or "Let's say a special prayer for the Anderson's sick baby" is the best knee-side education a youngster can get.

* **Instruction in the Faith.** If Catholic education is not available or affordable, insist that your youngster faithfully attend religious instruction. This will let your child know how important being Catholic is to you — and the education will serve to reinforce and aid in your parenting.

One seventh grader continually skipped his CCD evening class. When the teacher called the parent to inquire, the father quite bluntly told the teacher he felt his son's "hockey practice took precedence." At the end of hockey season, the boy returned but was cocky and disruptive. Unfortunately, this seventh grader learned from his dad that religion class was "no big deal."

* **Presenting the image of God.** Never forget that in your children's eyes you can do no wrong. *You are like God to them.* That thought alone should inspire every parent to ask for the Lord's guidance and grace to become the kind of image and guiding force needed to make big Catholics out of little ones.

# Chapter 8

# "And Baby Makes" . . . Jealousy

I was adopted at the age of nine months and enjoyed the undivided attention of my doting parents (who had gone eleven years without children before I arrived). My reign of glory abruptly ended at age three, however, when my parents adopted my brother.

I was so resentful, so the story goes, I dumped a load of encyclopedias on the unsuspecting three-month-old as he lay sleeping in his new crib. Fortunately, he was such a tough, stocky, little tyke (no wonder they nicknamed him "Butchie"), the only real damage done was to my backside and bruised ego.

Having a baby or adding another to your family can bring about all sorts of less-than-desirable responses from your other children. There's the "You-probably-won't-have-as-much-time-for-me" fear and the "Am I still your baby?" worry. Equally common is the feeling, "Oh no, he's here to stay." These feelings all fit under the umbrella of sibling rivalry. Thankfully, there's a grace period of about two months when baby does little more than eat, wet, and sleep and mom is running between "mop up," "heal up," and "catch up."

When sibling rivalry hits, however, it can be very disconcerting, often taking distracted parents completely by surprise. Actually, sibling rivalry is common and quite a natural tendency for youngsters who get bumped out of their rank by a new baby brother or sister.

"Just when we thought life was getting back to a normal routine," my friend Pat, a young mother of three confided, "the little spurts of jealousy seemed to reappear with Brian as Melissa began crawling and doing all those cute things that grab attention."

Disturbing as it may be, sibling rivalry is nothing new. It can be traced all the way back through history to the first and most noted example of Cain, who killed his brother Abel out of fierce envy. Jealousy then and now can show itself in many different ways.

My friend, Dorothy, called one day and in a puzzled voice described the behavior of Jennifer, the oldest of her four little ones. "I don't know what's wrong with her. When I ask what's bothering her, she says, 'Nothing,' and yet she cries at the drop of a pin. She is so helpful, dependable, and good and yet she seems so unhappy."

"The other day, I walked by the room with the baby and glanced over as Jenny and the others sat watching cartoons. Here was Jenny with tears streaming down her cheeks. Should I call the doctor?"

Jenny was too old to act naughty and so young to be the "big sister." She was feeling weighed down. "Just give her plenty of love and closeness during this busy adjustment period," I counseled, having been through it myself.

Poor little Jenny had a case of the "Am-I-still-your-baby-too?" and felt too responsible to show it any other way. Once she realized the cause, Dorothy immediately began lightening Jenny's heavy heart, with stronger measures of love and attention.

Dorothy not only showered Jenny with praise for her helpfulness around the home, but she spent an afternoon ALONE with Jenny shopping and then buying ice cream. The tears ceased.

In my own family, sibling jealousy has taken different forms with different children. Obviously by the time our thirteenth child, Joseph arrived, we had been through this a time or two, and yet we never managed to completely ward off the bent noses and green eyes that result from the arrival of the newest little bundle of love, looked on by some, as "the unwelcome invader."

Dominic, age three, and his older brother, Michael, age four, could not have been more loving toward baby Joseph. I told them they were my "helper boys," and constantly applauded every considerate gesture they made.

Dad took them on more errands, and even the older kids doubled their doses of hugs and attention, hoping they would not feel short-changed. I was proud of all of them. Our combined efforts seemed to work for the first few months.

The honeymoon was short-lived, however, as our peaceful co-existence and the helpfulness we once enjoyed turned gradually sour. About the time little Joseph turned five months old, and was stealing our hearts with his smiles and coos, the other two had decided they had had enough of mom and dad ogling and ahhing over every drool and coo the kid burped out.

Sweet-natured Michael began demanding that we help him dress and do things for him that he had previously taken great pride in doing for himself. His envy, however, paled in comparison to Dominic who had become so hyper and wild, I began to believe a day of ransacking with Atilla the Hun would have been more predictable.

So much for the months of positive reinforcement. And so much for all that "been-through-it-before" expertise. It had happened again.

What was our response? We again boosted the positive attention and came down firm on the negative. Wild and destructive behavior or pinching baby so the other kids will tell mom (as Dominic began to do) earned nothing better than a time-out period. I resisted the urge to spank and lecture because in Dominic's case, a spanking was also a form of attention and more welcome than removal from the fun zone.

On another occasion, one of our younger children, a sweet, though sometimes temperamental, seven-year-old, took a real nose dive with the arrival of a new baby sister. Up until then, she had never caused an ounce of trouble at school. Suddenly she became the class thief, sneaking back into the school during each day's recess period to lighten the lunch bags of her classmates by stealing all the cookies and treats.

Needless to say, we were shocked and baffled when the teacher called and told us what she was doing. Because this occurred right after Easter break, the first thing we did was to send her to school, Easter basket in hand, to distribute to all those she offended. In addition, she used savings to pay for the remainder of the stolen goodies.

On the other side, we realized we had quite a hurting little heart on our hands and so we doubled — no tripled — our efforts at love and affection. Once we realized what was going on, we hurt for her more than she did.

The incident of stealing never appeared in our youngster (now college-age) again. Attention and discipline do spell L O V E.

In this respect, children are so easy to please. It takes little effort to reassure them of our steadfast love. In fact, at such times parents must be careful to remember that there is a fine line between too much attention and not enough. An incident of a child showing a little natural envy and a need for more positive reinforcement, can be turned into a full-blown case of greed and demanding selfishness by an over-anxious, indulging parent.

About two months after the arrival of our second child, our sweet, even-natured first child (who up until then had been pure delight), began to occasionally throw temper tantrums. When we didn't respond after she spent several moments screaming, she would throw herself to the ground and hold her breath. I couldn't believe what came from that once charming little body.

In order to avoid the temptation of giving her the attention (either positive or negative) she sought, I would simply take my folded laundry, or cup of coffee, and casually walk into the other room. If she followed, I walked away again, until she got the message that this behavior goes no where with mom.

It's amazing how loved and wanted little ones feel if they are encouraged to demonstrate responsibility and reliability. Asking children to "go fer" this or "please can you get me that" is the best way to include them in your tasks and to praise them for their helpfulness.

When Michael was a baby, his big sisters, Kari and Angela (then two and four), became overly affectionate. Eager to smother him with hugs and kisses. The old adage of wanting to "squeeze him to death" best described the situation. We made a conscious effort to increase the cuddle periods with equal proportions of "go fer" jobs.

Such "go fer" compliments will also help offset those times when you are forced to discipline for jealous, out-of-control behavior. No matter how understandable, no temper tantrum, unruly demand, whining, or mean-spirited act should be ignored. It will only get worse.

A case in point: Occasionally children will demonstrate jealousy by slapping, pinching, or biting a new baby. A distraught mother once wrote to John Rosemond, a columnist who writes a feature on parenting.

She asked how to keep her three-year-old daughter from hurting her ten-month-old son. The woman wrote, "The usual scenario begins with her picking him up to 'love' him. Then she squeezes too hard or pinches his cheek, and he starts crying. When we reprimand her, she always says she's sorry and acts contrite. We are baffled. Is she doing this on purpose?"

Rosemond recommended that the mother place the baby "off-limits" to the older child for a period of one or two weeks. He suggested she tell the child this time-out period is needed until the girl can learn ways to be gentle and loving toward the baby.

"When a privilege is withheld from someone, that privilege looks increasingly attractive. By keeping your daughter at a distance from her brother, contact with him becomes more desirable," Rosemond wrote. The mom was told to use the training period to encourage the daughter's helpfulness, yet avoid all contact and touching. After the "off-limits" time had expired, the child was permitted brief and supervised contact with the baby. "Let her give him a spoonful of cereal," Rosemond suggested, or "let her hold him on her lap."

Rosemond contends that by withholding the privilege of physical touching and interaction with the baby, the child will learn what a privilege it is and will want to regain the privilege as well as the parents' trust.

No matter what form sibling jealousy takes, it's important for parents to remember patience, praise, and perseverance in their love and discipline. Incidents of resentment may come and go but the trying times will end sooner if the child is praised often and never pampered or passed-over.

Envy is a sin and it is up to us as Christian parents to teach our children to curb and control such hurtful feelings. Yet Paul also tells us in Romans that "all things work for good for those who love God, who are called according to his purpose" (Romans 8:28). In that regard we might pray that signs of jealousy in family life may be turned into opportunities of goodness.

The story of Cain and Abel in Genesis 4:1-8 ended in tragedy with the murder of Abel because of his brother Cain's uncontrollable envy. But the story of Joseph (Genesis 37:28) who was sold to the Ishmaelites for "twenty pieces of silver" by his eleven brothers, shows a different ending. Although the brothers meant to harm Joseph because of their fierce jealousy, God turned the situation around for good.

Sold as a slave, Joseph became an Egyptian ruler and made preparations for protecting the people from starving during a famine. Instead of using his new status to seek revenge on his unsuspecting, destitute brothers, Joseph took pity on their plight. He provided them with needed food and forgave them.

Perhaps parents will never successfully ward off sibling jealousy. But then again, perhaps we may not want to. Perhaps it's time we view sibling rivalry as an opportunity to help our children learn lessons in self-control, acceptance, obedience, remorse for wrong-doing, and best of all, love.

# Chapter 9

# My Kids Are Spoiled

There's no denying it. My kids are spoiled. No matter how hard we've tried, and in spite of our family size, they're spoiled. Maybe not "spoiled rotten," as the saying goes, but nonetheless they're spoiled.

Raising thirteen children in a single-income household has not been without sacrifice, and even though our children grew up sharing bedrooms, toys, hand-me-down clothes, and just about everything imaginable, there is nothing they *need*.

Like most parents, we want the best for our children. We want them to grow up feeling loved and secure. (After all, what kind of parent would deliberately DEPRIVE a child?) We have tried to lay a solid foundation by setting good standards and establishing firm family rules. "Rights and responsibilities go hand in hand," we have often preached, as we assigned household chores to all but the very youngest of our brood.

As our children grew, we allowed them to discover firsthand, the thrill of thrift, money management, and small business ventures, by working as baby-sitters and paper carriers, doing lawn and snow-shoveling jobs, and eventually working part-time employment. They weren't always impressed!

Nevertheless, there were many occasions when it took commitment and nerves of steel to resist the urging, begging, pleading, and pouting that would have pampered their every whim.

My children think they know deprivation just because they grew up on powdered milk, washed dishes by hand, rode in secondhand cars, watched television on a set older than most of them, wore other kids' clothes, and were "the last ones" on earth to get a VCR — thanks to the generosity of Grandma K. They're spoiled!

Our youngsters, like most of the kids of today, have EVERYTHING, and if they don't, with very little effort — they can.

"The problem we have in parenting is trying to deny our children in an environment that has too much. They will never become *givers* if they're accustomed to being *takers*," my husband John recently told a television producer who called inviting his input for an upcoming program on positive parenting.

"Even so-called poor children in America are far more affluent than the children of the Third World," John continued. "Children of the Third World suffer from poverty of the body and mind, as they are deprived of the bare essentials of food, shelter, medical care, and even minimal education. The poor of America suffer from a poverty of the soul and spirit as the affluence and greed surrounding them work to encourage a lust — not for eternal happiness — but material and carnal desires."

Even Christians in a secular world often fail to heed Christ's words in Luke: 12:23, 30-31 "For life is more than food and the body more than clothing. . . . All the nations of the world seek for these things, and your father knows that you need them. Instead, seek his kingdom, and these other things will be given you besides."

Yet, in fairness, being spoiled is not our youngsters' fault. The spoiling began with us — their parents. We were the baby-boomers, the 60s kids, who had time to be hippies, time to "drop out" of society, time to go to college, and time to be young. We were the most pampered of generations, never fretting about being forced into child labor or measured by the work we could produce.

We knew nothing more about a depression than what our school texts or reminiscing parents told us. We don't have the remotest idea of what it would be like to wait for something or to really "go without." We never owned a ration card, or waited in a line for hours for a piece of meat or a loaf of bread.

We grew up on TV, frozen foods, take-home pizzas, automatic dishwashers, hair dryers, air-conditioning, and family cars. With little effort, most of us owned a bicycle, radio, stereo, and for some — a car of our own. In addition, we enjoyed more leisure time than any generation before us — until our kids, that is.

I remember my mother-in-law's nostalgia at spotting a picture of her husband in an old Depression-era newspaper photo depicting hundreds of Minnesotans standing in overcoats and winter apparel in slightly-above-zero weather, as they waited to buy a pair of nylon stockings. "Dad waited for hours in line just to surprise me with one pair," she said. "Though the nylon was heavy and far from sheer, we women were just grateful then to have anything close to a nylon stocking to wear."

Waiting in lines? The only comparable memories we, or our kids, have, is waiting in line for a sports event or sell-out concert!

Our pampered generation grew up in an era of neighborhood schools — no "walking five miles" for us — and stay-at-home mothers who packed our lunches and cared for our every need. Granted, many, like my father, took on a second job "to make ends meet." But that was done in order to afford not the essentials, but the extras — a room addition, a new piano, a cabin up north, a family vacation, college or a private education, a second car or secondhand boat. If our parents made one mistake it was in their desire to give their children what they "never had." We were spoiled.

Yet, growing up back then, in the 40s, 50s, and early 60s, we were made to feel there was a future just waiting for us, if we just had the gumption and drive to roll up our sleeves and make it happen.

Work and incentive — perhaps THAT's what we forgot to give our kids in our rush to give them everything. **Today's children have not been made to feel there is important work waiting for them and that their contribution in life WILL make a positive difference. In**

**Christian terms, we call this a vocation.**

We must instill the concept that "Whistle while you work" brings more happiness and fulfillment than "You deserve a break today" and "Have it your way."

Speaking of today's youth, one fast-food employer said, "We're lucky if we can keep some of them for six months. The turn-over is tremendous as kids come and go, searching for a job they 'like.'" Living in a society with more work than workers, the teens of today — unlike the generations before them who were grateful just to be working — can oftentimes name their price and their hours.

"They have money in their pockets and can buy any little trinket they want, regardless of whether or not they're paying for their own expenses and education," Dan, a father of three, lamented.

Do today's kids *need* to work? About as much as I need a Cadillac. Yet there's nothing like good, old-fashioned work to build character and self-esteem. It gives young people drive and helps them channel that boundless energy toward something productive and rewarding. "An idle brain is the devil's workshop," so goes an old proverb.

More to the point, English author Hannah More once wrote, "A man who is able to employ himself innocently is never miserable. It is the idle who are wretched. If I wanted to inflict the greatest punishment on a fellow-creature I would shut him alone in a dark room without employment. Idleness among children, as among men, is the root of all evil. . . ."

One day Tina came home from high school trying not to be envious as she described a fellow classmate, "who never had a job and whose parents give her an allowance and buy her EVERYTHING." Tina, who had had a paper route since she was eleven and then went on to babysitting and part-time employment in order to pay for her own clothing, expenses, and ultimately her college tuition, was understandably jealous until I reminded her about what she had that her friend did not.

"You have your freedom, your independence, and the

pride in knowing that the clothes you wear, the places you go, and the school you will attend are yours because you earned it," I told Tina. "Your poor friend has to ask for every nickel she has, and is totally dependent upon the generosity of her parents. What a rude awakening it will be when she can no longer run to others for help."

"There is a pride that can only come when you've worked for something you badly want," I relayed to her. "It brings a feeling of accomplishment your poor friend can't yet comprehend." I'm not sure Tina bought it!

America's young are growing up in the most plentiful era of this nation's history. Such times, however, have also produced a generation of troubled, confused, and unhappy adolescents.

It is estimated that each year one hundred thousand children in our nation are placed in hospitals or residential treatment centers where attempts are made to cure, care for, or at least control, out-of-control destructive behavior or prevent continued flirtation with drugs, overeating, suicide, sexual promiscuity and, even criminal behavior.

Since 1970, juvenile admissions to psychiatric hospitals are up sixfold; for residential treatment centers, figures show at least a twofold increase.

What can we do as parents who love our kids and want the best for them?

We can't move, we can't put a bag over their heads, and we can't ignore what's meant to entice and seduce our young. But we can be firm, and we can love our youngsters enough to say, "No" to them, and to ration some of those goods and privileges.

Perhaps the best place to begin is with ourselves, letting our youngsters see that we willingly make sacrifices, over and above our charitable contributions, to enhance the lives and welfare of others. **We must let them SEE that we do what we do for the love of God**. Children will only understand the meaning and practice of personal discipline and self-restraint if they see their parents and adult mentors — teachers, aunts and uncles, neighbors and friends —

doing the same. We must show prudence in our eating, drinking, entertainment, and appetite for luxuries, if we expect our children to do the same. Like it or not, we are their greatest role models.

In the long run, we do them no favor when we give in to their desires and demands — even if it promises to "keep peace" and prevent a standoff. Unless we offer a healthy mixture of love and discipline to the adults of tomorrow (our kids) they are doomed to become the most intolerant, self-centered, demanding, and self-directed generation of Americans ever — a legacy of unhappiness — certain to do themselves and others harm.

Work and incentive, sacrifice and self-restraint — keys to building strong character and self-esteem. Let's love our children enough to deprive them!

# Chapter 10

# Going On Vacation And Surviving

John has always insisted we get away ALONE at least once each year. He calls it "an investment on our marriage." Spoken like a true accountant! This helps keep a marriage strong and unified. It also renews a tone of intimacy and fun that is so vital in every married couple's relationship. John teasingly tells the kids, however, that we're "doing it for them."

"The more in love and happier mom and dad are, the more love and happiness we can give to you." The kids may not fully understand it, but it works! We likewise believe a vacation with the entire family is important. Which is easier said than done with our rainbow collection of children.

Through past experiences, we have become staunch advocates of all-family vacations, and we have witnessed the unifying love and shared memories such getaways provide.

All but the very youngest help pack and prepare for the upcoming event — our once-a-year holiday. By the day of departure, each child has saved enough money from paper routes, babysitting, lawn and snow shoveling, or part-time jobs to help finance the trip's expense. We pay the lodging, travel, and meal costs. The children ante up for their own personal souvenirs, amusement park fees, etc.

This arrangement has lightened our burden considerably. It also has helped our boys and girls become responsible and thrifty shoppers. It's surprising what they decide to do without when they are the ones paying.

Theresa once did without the water-squirting corsage from Wall Drug. Mary Elizabeth sacrificed the glow-in-the-dark musical reproduction of Mount Rushmore. Tony put back the can of rubber snakes. Tim and Charlie, our unpredictable teens, stifled the urge to bring home the "authentic Buffalo Chips" for Grandma and Grandpa. (Not everyone appreciates such humor!)

We have stopped counting how many times people have asked us what club, church, or camp we are from. I've also learned to resist the temptation to reply: "Mission Mutiny" or "Camp Dysentery." Instead I merely ask the shortest route to the next set of WORKING toilets.

Not being campers, nor people of means, we have spent most of our vacation nights in ONE motel room. In fact, it's often been that daily goal of a room and pool (a vital necessity) that has kept our youngsters willing to endure hearing their father say hour after hour, "Let's just see if we can make it a little farther."

Sleeping in one room is a story all its own. In our case, the floor usually looked like a mini-bomb shelter with lanky teens and wiggly toddlers wrestling for every inch of floor space.

Among our group are two loud thumb suckers, one noisy finger smacker, one teeth-grinding seven-year-old, two snorers, and one sleep-talker. Oftentimes, our son with hearing aids was the only one who slept through it all. He just tuned out the whole mess.

To economize, we picnic at roadside stops. It's been fun to boast of our lunches in the Badlands, the Grand Canyon, Disneyland, the Utah Salt Flats and Colorado Rockies. Those to be forgotten are the ones behind gas stations, during a Nebraska hail storm, in the middle of a Santa Ana wind storm, with the ants in the peanut butter jar, or the time we backed over the bag in the parking lot on a day we hadn't eaten for five hours.

On occasion, we splurge and eat out. Humility is often a virtue developed on such excursions. There was the time Tina, Charlie, and Vincent ordered liver and onions, and the others boycotted their table, all holding their noses as the waitress passed by to deliver their meal.

On another trip, during a day-long drive we found ourselves on a lonely stretch of freeway with no lunch and little to share. The kids were dining on warm grapes, melted marshmallows (it was ninety degrees in the shade), one all-day sucker (coated with sand and dirt from its previous home in the bottom of the diaper bag), and whatever soda crackers and cookies they could scrape from between the car seats.

When we spotted the sign "Dine at Lucky's," we eagerly pulled in. Imagine our disappointment when we discovered that Lucky's was nothing but a greasy-spoon pit (and I do mean "pit") stop, that charged four times the going rate for every selection on the eight item menu. With fourteen tired, hungry, and very claustrophobic people, we could wait no longer. We ordered fourteen ($4.95 each) Lucky's grilled cheese sandwiches (no fries, slaw, pickle, or even a parsley flake) and resisted the urge to eat more.

Since Lucky's was the only diner for miles, other travelers were routinely caught in the same pay-or-famish dilemma. Our older children began timing how long it took new customers to leave once they spotted the solid-gold price list and the finished products (some were not all that finished). Chrissy, Tim, Charlie, and Tina (our fearless four-some), wanted to make picket signs and hold them up for potential victims, warning, "Dining at Lucky's could be your most expensive, if not your LAST, meal."

With each of our adventures, we have really had far more delight than difficulty and have almost become used to hearing, "Are we there, yet?" — "I can't hold it" — "I'm telling!" — or worst of all — "I smell something."

All things considered, we nevertheless, heartily recommend such travel. For those planning their very first trip here are a few lessons we've learned over the years:

### DO'S:
* *Travel with those you love.* It helps you resist the temptation to throw someone out the window or leave an ornery member at a remote rest area.

* *Everyone must prepare and save for the trip.* Even the very young can sacrifice a little spending money in anticipa-

tion. The vacation then becomes important to all.

* *Plan ahead.* Unless you are adventuresome and don't mind sleeping outdoors with bugs, wild animals, or fresh-fallen snow — phone ahead for reservations, keeping alternate spots in mind. And don't forget to remind the family "lead foot" that this is a vacation, NOT the Indy 500 race.

* *A laugh and a prayer each day.* This helps keep that flat-tire experience, the forgotten underwear, locked car doors in ninety-eight degree heat with no extra keys, and the carload of carsick children in perspective. Convince yourself that unless you see blood or death — you are having a wonderful time.

* *A family in a moving car is a captive audience.* What better time to thank our Creator (and ask Him to help us find where Dominic put the road maps). A Rosary a day takes care of just about any crisis.

### BE SURE TO BRING:
* *Vitamins - for you.* NOT the children.
* *Some surprises for the little ones.* A dime-store truck or a tiny hand-holding dolly will keep a child busy for hours because the item is new and different. Great for that second or third long day of driving.

### DON'TS:
* *Don't forget an extra set of car keys, phone numbers, and addresses.* Ever since my husband waited in one hundred ten-degree Arizona heat while I browsed through six Phoenix phone books, I have remembered to bring the addresses.

* *Don't forget the First Aid kit.* Also, remember the soap (laundry and dishes), toilet paper (trust me), rags, litter bags, labeled cups and eating utensils (good for the economy and ecology).

* *Don't consider this your second honeymoon or that "trip you always wanted to take."* When traveling with children, consider it more their holiday than yours. This way, if you do find yourself having fun, it's such a nice

surprise, and you're not as frustrated when they tell you they'd rather read *Mad* Magazine or play cards, than watch another shooting geyser at Yellowstone Park.

### An Exception To Every Rule:

Many years after one family trip, our older children discovered that baby sister, Kari, was conceived in Colorado. After we survived the usual, "Mother, how could you?" we told them our rendezvous reunion was a parental privilege, reminding them, however, that staying up late to do laundry does have its pluses.

* *Don't listen to everything the children say.* If their bickering is getting to you, consider it their offer to help. Let them do all the dishes, garbage and car clean-up for the day.

* *Don't pack much — wash often.* Be sure to watch for any unusual "souvenirs" — especially those that melt, grow, shed, mold, or CRAWL.

Beware of smugglers who never admit they packed the pet lizard, the pregnant gerbil, or the open can of dog food at the bottom of the lunchmeat container.

### Remember:

This is not the time to potty train your toddler, to begin a new diet, to quit smoking, to teach your eager teen how to practice behind-the-wheel driving, to wean yourself from high blood pressure medication, or to cancel your mental health coverage.

An all-family vacation is just the time for fun, faith, and LOVE.

# Chapter 11

# Impressions On The Young

Our twelve-passenger van was loaded from floorboard to
window panes with comics and kids, as we bravely headed
for the state of California on what is now fondly remembered by all (we had only ten kids at the time) as the biggest and most fun-filled vacation ever.

So as not to tire the children or our temperamental old
car, we made frequent stops, taking in the particular sights
and sounds, parkways, and picnic areas, not to mention the
gas stations and restrooms we encountered on our route.
Stopping to visit with relatives and old friends along the
way, each day brought us closer to our destination and a
host of new memories.

One of our favorite vacation things to do is to begin the
day with morning Mass. As a result we've been to liturgies
in log cabins, church basements, and elegant Cathedrals.
We've prayed while surrounded by the grandeur of the
Colorado Rockies and during hailstorms in Nebraska —
each Mass and locale taking on a meaning all its own.

We found it was not only a wonderful way to show our
gratitude to a generous Heavenly Father, but even more, it
made us feel we had a special part in — even a closeness to,
in some situations — the lives of people we met along the
way in the different locations. On more than one occasion,
our youngsters were impressed by the faith and devotion of
others.

In Colorado, there were sheep farmers with their
modern-day trucks herding hundreds of grazing sheep. Yet
set off in a cove, visible to the shepherds, and even the most
distracted highway motorist, was a shrine adorned with
glitter and lights surrounding a small statue of the Blessed
Mother. Yes, shepherds still pray in the twentieth century!

While visiting an aunt and uncle in a small California suburb, we had the privilege of attending a Mass at which the songs, prayers, and even the homily was in Spanish, to our youngsters delight!

These are the occasions when it is a special joy to be Catholic and to realize that no matter where you go, the Sacrifice of the Mass, in whatever language, is the same powerful prayer.

On another occasion, while in a small Arizona town, we showed up just after the consecration (thanks to an outdated yellow pages which posted the wrong Mass schedule), only to see the priest pass out the counted hosts to the less than twenty participants. The communicants, the majority of whom were Indian and elderly, turned to see our line up of disappointed youngsters and without hesitation began breaking their hosts so as to share with this family of twelve who had barged in on their liturgy. The kids were so touched. Surely Our Lord smiled that sun-filled June day at those thoughtful, giving hearts.

The children, who were not always eager to begin their vacation days by rolling out of bed early for Mass, nevertheless, still recall some of the funny events our going to Mass triggered. Once an elderly nun came rushing after us as we departed an inner-city cathedral asking if we were part of a new "refugee migration" of families they were waiting to host and enroll in their school. "No," we politely told her. "We are all one family and our Asian, Black, Hispanic, Indian, and Caucasian children, though different in appearance, are related by adoption, if not by blood."

At another stop, one of our boys was mistaken for a tardy altar boy and would have been properly dressed down by waiting clergy, if dad hadn't come through the door just in time.

On several occasions, we were nabbed by curious onlookers intrigued by our numbers who asked if we were part of a Scout troop or children's foster camp. Our kids, the older of whom claim embarrassment by the attention, nonetheless, relish the comical spotlight.

One of the lessons we keep learning as parents is just how much children notice — including those who claim not to be interested.

At one Colorado metropolitan city we awoke early and drove across town to the cathedral for the liturgy. Upon entering the church, however, we were informed by a woman custodian that "today is Father's day off. Sorry. No Mass." So much for believing posted signs on Church lawns.

Certainly every priest deserves and NEEDS a day to himself and with the current clergy shortage, most are over-worked and overwhelmed. This is hard to explain to youngsters who have just given up another day to sleep in, however. Especially when they spotted two priests in the church parking lot, placing golf bags in a car trunk. "Couldn't they have said Mass first?" our Charlie mumbled.

On several occasions during our twenty-one-day trip a celebrant was flanked by two lip-glossed, pierced-earringed altar girls. My boys (three of whom were altar boy ages) im-mediately spotted the discrepancy. "Aren't they being dis-obedient to the Pope?" our own disobedient-prone son, Tim, asked. What's a parent to say?

Perhaps the most unfortunate incident along the route was the morning Mass we attended in Nebraska. The of-ficiating priest rushed through the words in a hurried, al-most irreverent manner. He was so obviously irritated that when the Mass ended and we were walking out, our son Tony said, "Boy, that priest sure hates his job."

We struggled to find words to excuse the un-priestly manner we had witnessed. We suggested that perhaps the middle-aged priest had just heard some terrible news or was having a bad day (which we all do). The children be-came all the more adamant, however, in their belief that he angrily rushed through the Mass because to him it was a monotonous and boring "job."

As we drove from Nebraska to Arizona that heated day, I prayed, "Lord these are your kids and I know you love them far more than we do. We want them to love the faith and perhaps even consider the priesthood or religious life themselves, but they never will if they think that a day of golf takes precedence for some priests, while others appear to dislike the chosen vocation altogether."

As luck would have it, our travel day ended abruptly with the car breaking down in Kayenta, Arizona. Located on an Indian reservation, the only signs of life we saw were four gas stations, a newly built supermarket, an Indian Trade store, a motel (thank the Lord!), and a tiny Catholic Church. We stayed the night while our car was being repaired.

The next morning we awoke and dressed early. We drove along the dusty road to the small, but attractive, Navajo mission church. Taking up two rows that early weekday morning, the only other churchgoers were an elderly Indian woman, a nun, and a father and son.

The priest took his unconsecrated hosts from a plastic margarine container and reverently placed them on the simple altar. He devoutly said the Mass, encouraging all to sing, as if his congregation were at St. Peters in Rome. During the homily, he joyfully announced that this day began his thirty-fifth year as an ordained priest.

"I am so grateful to God for calling me to this vocation. There has not been one day that I have not been thankful for the blessings my priestly ministry has brought me," he said.

What a contrast from the morning before. Here was a man surrounded by desert and deprivation and yet he possessed an abundance of happiness and exuberant love for the Lord. The other priest, the angry one, who *appeared* to have so much more with his lovely large church building, gorgeous statutes, and abundant staff and school, left our children with the impression that the priesthood is just a job.

The Arizona mission priest, who had little by comparison, reminded us that the priesthood is a vocation — a call from God on high and an opportunity to serve His people.

The incident reminded us too, of how much God's people

should be praying for vocations and for ALL of the priests who faithfully serve us, so that they are never discouraged or tempted to treat their priestly call as just a job.

# The Sisters

Catherine 6

*Chapter 12*

# Our White "Knight"
# Every Large Family
# Should Have One

I wish everyone could experience the wonderful Catholic nuns I have experienced. In my youth I had nuns as teachers, advisers, counselors, and comforters. They made a positive and lasting impression on my life. As a mom of many, I now see the Sisters have assumed a more varying role in our community. Capturing no headlines and making no news, still their Christ-like presence has transformed thousands upon thousands of individual lives.

A wonderful case in point is Sister Stephen - whom my children affectionately call "The White knight," because of the way she seems to drive up "out of nowhere" honking her car horn until we run out to the curb, where she then plops her "bargain" of goodies — and off she goes again.

I first met this seventy-five-year-old nun the day I delivered Angela Marie, our eighth child. As I lay in the recovery room after giving birth, Sister burst past the "No Visitors Allowed" sign and flustered nursing staff, to present me with a handful of fresh-cut roses — snipped from the pastor's garden. (I learned later that if Father wants to see his flowers in bloom, he must look out the rectory window early each morning before Sister Stephen comes with her scissors.) Sister says roses "are for people" — especially her shut-ins.

Sister Stephen believes flowers are "essential" in her ministry to shut-ins. Late one evening, while I went for a walk, I discovered how she obtains her bouquets when Father's garden isn't providing, and there are none to be begged from others. It was shortly after dark as I caught

Sister sneaking in the side door of church. She tiptoed up to the main altar and after reverently genuflecting, she began to pull out a few daisies, mums and ferns from each of the two large sprays behind the altar.

She warned me not to tell, realizing how it would displease her convent companion, Sister Antonelle, who had to care for the altar and decorations. After leaving the church, Sister carefully placed the flowers in two coffee cans around the side of the convent, to avoid provoking a normally serene and good-natured Sister Antonelle.

The morning after Sister Stephen's late-night caper, a parishioner rang the convent doorbell, interrupting the nuns at breakfast, to report, "Someone must have brought you some flowers early this morning and left them in cans around the side of the conventhouse."

Before the others could move, Sister Stephen jumped to her feet, and exclaimed: "Thank you, Lord! Just what I need for my people today. I'll deliver them right away!"

And off she went.

Sister bargains with EVERYONE — including the saints. When she heard St. Anthony still hadn't answered her prayers "to find employment" for a young, out-of-work father (with five children), she confided, "I know what he's waiting for. He wants me to fast over this, and I still owe him a day from the last favor. I guess I better get to it."

Because of a serious heart condition, Sister is supposed to be semi-retired, with a "limited ministry." Yet, on occasion, Father has had to order her "grounded" to prevent her from going out in penetrating heat or snowstorms in order to serve those she affectionately calls "my people."

Rumor has it that she almost got a speeding ticket once, but when the cop pulled her over and saw it was Sister Stephen with a back seat and trunk loaded down with day-old breads and rolls, he just gave her a stern warning and wished her well.

Sister has her daily list of shut-ins to call on, hospitals to visit and individuals in need. She spends time with each, making them feel they are the most important part of her day. Besides bringing them Holy Communion, she prays with them, talks with them, and loves them. If they have other needs — financial, emotional, babysitting, doctors' appointments, escorts to church or just car rides, Sister makes the arrangements.

In addition to her care of the sick, poor or elderly, she has "adopted" many families like ours. Our family certainly can't be classified as being among those living in abject poverty, but because of our sheer numbers, and the financial budget we must therefore adhere to, Sister has decided we could use a "little special attention." Thus, we are, on occasion, lavished with a ham, turkey, canned vegetables, fruit, day-old breads, rolls, or cookies and crackers obtained from nearby stores or manufacturing plants.

Some say Sister is more con than saint because she has been known to manipulate, plead, badger, and beg for whatever it is she wants. It's NEVER for herself, however, but ALWAYS for "her people."

I know of Protestants who send her annual donations. She once lectured the manager of a local fast-food restaurant for not doing anything for the poor in our area. When the man told her that the parent corporation had donated to charitable causes, she retorted: "That's not good enough. What about MY people right here who would love to taste one of your hamburgers and shakes?" He relented, and gave her some coupons to give to her families.

Name a merchant or grocer in this community, and he's been touched by Sister Stephen — in more ways than one.

Sometimes, Sister brings us a birthday cake (even when it's no one's birthday). It may be a day or two old or have someone else's name on it, but we're always very grateful for the baker's mistake in spelling or color decoration — and for the little nun who begs on our behalf. We never had a store-bought cake at our house till Sister Stephen joined our parish staff.

Sister has a special affection for children — especially the handicapped or "less than perfect." She takes them for rides, brings them treats, and always seems to single them out for attention. Or, is it they who single her out? One day, she called and invited some of my little ones to HER birthday party. When the children returned they told of eating a scrumptious cake and ice cream in the convent dining room (no less) and of all the treats and goodies Sister had hidden for them throughout the convent house — a birthday they won't forget.

When Kari was born two years after Angela, she was so terribly jaundiced she had to be re-hospitalized for three days. We were very worried. It was Mother's Day, and I spent the time in tears at her side watching her little, yellow body in the lighted isolette. When Sister Stephen heard the news, she was there within hours.

She came storming down the hospital corridor carrying a soggy brown paper sack which dripped with every step. When she opened the bag, she pulled out an eight-inch-high plastic holy water statue of St. Anthony. My non-Christian roommate (a young, first-time mother whose child was also ill) looked on in utter shock as she watched the nun pull Kari from the enclosed cubicle and gently lay her on a nearby bed, sprinkling the child, bed, and surroundings with the blessed water, and pleading for St. Anthony's prayers and the Lord's healing, "quickly, so this baby and mother can be home with their family."

Three hours later, when the nurse came in to take another blood test to reassess the Bilirubin count, my roommate's child's condition remained unchanged. Kari's count had dropped a radical six points. We were discharged the following morning as our hospital-room partners stayed on.

A merchant once told Sister Stephen he could get her some turkeys (but nothing else) for Thanksgiving.

A week later, she presented him with a list of her wants, which included a number of turkeys, chickens, and small roasts. He shook his head in protest and said, "Turkeys, Sister, I told you. All I can get is turkeys."

Ignoring his declaration, the nun begged, "But some of my people can't eat turkey, so, they must have something else."

Refusing to take "No" for an answer, she confidently told the man she would send a parishioner around on Tuesday for her items.

Who could refuse Sister Stephen? On Tuesday, her list of "wants" was ready.

Sister is not known to pay full price for anything. If she can't get it for free, she uses coupons or she bargains, begs, and then convinces her trapped seller that she is still entitled to her "five-percent clergy discount."

When my parents celebrated their fiftieth wedding anniversary, Sister knew I wanted to have something very special for them, although funds were limited. Before my guest list was even complete, she was dropping off bags of groceries to lighten the family budget, so we could make room for the extra costs involved. In telling her of my party plans for the event one afternoon, I mentioned my wish for some "nice fresh-cut flowers" as table arrangements around the house.

Three days before our open house, the phone rang, and I heard a voice on the other end say, "Well, I've contacted three funeral homes so far, but no one has died, yet. As soon as they do, the funeral directors will save me the leftover flowers."

It was Sister Stephen, and sure enough, the day before our anniversary party, Sister had four huge sprays delivered to our home.

Our out-of-town guests who were staying with us looked a little stunned when they first arrived and saw the flowers with ribbons proclaiming "Grandfather," "Brother," and "Son," but by the following morning, anniversary day, we had neatly rearranged them into lovely small table bouquets, with only a few of us knowing where the flowers had actually come from. Thank heavens for Sister Stephen and her "connections."

At First Communion time, some of our young were outfitted, from head to toe, in a beautiful white lace dress and veil — compliments of you-know-who. When we finished with the outfit, we cleaned it, packaged it up and returned it to Sister for the next eager communicant on her list.

Though far from poor, we have experienced our desperate moments over the years. There was the time our Tony lost his retainer (replacement cost — $350.00). The morning after Sister heard, she pressed $50.00 in my palm during the handshake of peace, and assured me that St. Anthony had already heard from her.

There were more events like that than I can name, including the times we've been faced with bills for two hearing aids for Vincent, braces for Tim, a new roof, tuition and mortgage, all seeming to come due at once. In each instance, Sister Stephen, often without knowing our specific need, was there with "a little something" which got us over the rough spots.

News stories have recently surfaced revealing that our elderly nuns or their orders are in serious financial need. After the decades of goodness they have spread throughout this land, it seems only fitting that we could do at least "a little something" for those who have dedicated their lives to Christ and to us — "His people."

# Grandparents
Angela. Kuharski. Age. 9

Grandpa          Grandma

# Chapter 13

# Grandma's Lesson:
# A Deeper Meaning To Life

By today's standards, my grandma would have been a perfect candidate for a nursing home — or worse. She had had several small strokes, was hard of hearing (rarely wearing an aid because she thought it "bulky"), exhibited periods of forgetfulness and senility, and had a frightening habit of wandering. (The police brought her home on more than one occasion. She once turned up in Milwaukee, Wisconsin, and someone had to drive from Minneapolis to get her.)

In my early years, I remember Grandma for the hours of poetry and fun stories she could recite from memory, for her wonderful Dandelion Greens Salad (which we picked and prepared together), for her medicinal "home remedies" that healed and soothed, and, most of all, for those marvelous bus excursions which took us through town to experience sights and sounds I had never known before. When I was with Grandma, I knew I was in for adventure.

As she grew older, she changed and could no longer live alone — needing to be "watched," a humbling judgment for this once strong and still proud German mother of eight. God bless my folks and aunts and uncles who took turns hosting Grandma in their homes, believing it was important that she be with family.

I was fortunate, though I didn't always realize it then, to share my bed and room with Grandma. This was God's gift to keep this "only daughter" from becoming selfish, snobbish, and self-indulgent. While I ALMOST got used to her loud snoring, her insistence on using a "chamber pot" under our shared double bed more than tried my teenage tolerance. Poor Grandma. She was merely trying to avoid the long flight of stairs down to the only bathroom in the house.

She became more senile with age, and yet, we children still saw her as fun to be with, even enjoying her eccentricities. We delighted in the way she would hide her dentures (she hated to wear them) in drawers, cupboards, drinking glasses, or potted plants, and then "forget" where she put them when mom asked her to put them in for church or a shopping trip.

Grandma carried AT LEAST two shopping bags with her at all times, and I loved to see what was packed inside. Once in a while, there would be some candy or trinket, but mostly I recall the old newspapers, twine, magazines, hairbrushes (used on her long grey hair), and bits of clothing.

Thinking back, those bags were loaded with pretty worthless and crazy items, though I didn't think so then, because I knew they were important to Grandma. Today, she would be described as a "bag lady," but to us she was Grandma.

She had a way of collecting, or taking, things that didn't belong to her and then giving them to someone else. I'll never forget my adolescent outrage the morning I awoke to find her gone (on the early bus), along with MY new hairbrush, new school blouse and matching skirt. Later, I heard the items turned up as "gifts" for my cousin, Beverly. Grandma merely explained that Beverly, coming from a large family, needed the clothes much more than I. She was right.

One time, Grandma failed to turn off the gas burner after frying pork chops in the middle of the night. We had extensive smoke damage throughout the house — not to mention a frightful scare. I remember mom and dad being terribly upset, but there was never talk of getting rid of Grandma. We just watched her more closely.

In spite of her senility, Grandma still had an uncanny way of making me believe I was actually "becoming quite a lovely young lady," in spite of the awkward, pimple-faced girl with the lanky legs and AAA figure I saw reflected in the bedroom mirror.

I'll remember her most, not for her erratic, insane antics, but for the moments of tenderness, affection, and love that seemed to seep through, no matter what other changes were more visible in her aging frame. The instance that stands out the most occurred when I was sixteen and working nights at a local drive-in restaurant.

In the winter months, I'd get off late and pour my half-frozen body into bed next to Grandma. Feeling my presence, and yet not being able to converse because of her hearing disability, she would get up and take hold of first my hands, and then my icy feet, gently rubbing them with her feeble fingers until they were warm to her touch. In essence, she became cold to provide me warmth.

Even as a saucy teen I felt humbled and undeserving to have this grey-haired and weary old woman stooping over to care for me, when I knew it should have been I who stooped to care for her.

Grandma's last months of life were spent in a hospital following a stroke which left her paralyzed and comatose. Her children came from far-away states to see her, but she gave no visible sign that she was aware of their presence. No one talked, however, of pulling the plug of her respirator, or discontinuing her feeding, or suggested she was no longer "meaningful." She was still Grandma.

Grandma died before my seventeenth birthday. No other death has caused such an emptiness in me.

In 1986, the American Medical Association declared it was ethical for doctors to withhold all means of life-prolonging medical treatment, including food and water, from irreversibly comatose patients, even if death IS NOT imminent (emphasis mine). Since then, many court cases have resulted in the legal starvation deaths of patients who were severely brain-damaged; patients who could see, hear, respond to touch and pain, some of them young, none of them DYING. Have advocates of death-by-someone's-choice not seen the painful and horrifying sight of a person left to die by starvation and dehydration? Have they not heard the teaching of Jesus: "Whenever you neglect even the least of your brethren, you neglect Me also"?

Increasingly we're hearing reports about organizations working to legalize "aid in dying" — death by lethal injection for "qualified patients." These organizations suggest Holland as a role model, where an estimated 6,000 to 18,000 patients die each year at the hands of doctors. They curiously ignore documented abuses: hospitals admitting they kill patients without consent, children with cancer provided with poisons, euthanasia "referral services," senior citizens terrorized by the prospect of being "done in" as a cost-containment measure, old folks refusing to drink their orange juice for fear it might be poisoned.

I thought again of Grandma and how such "progress" could have ended her life. More than that, I thought of how much I had learned about caring and unconditional love during those years through the Christ-like example of my parents, relatives, and the medical staff who looked after her. Compared to the AMA's death decree and Holland's promise of easy death, I think Grandma AND we had it so much better.

# Chapter 14

# Commitment

My mom and dad accomplished a feat not many of us will be able to match. I'm sure glad our family was around to see it. They celebrated their Golden Wedding Anniversary.

Fifty years — now that's commitment!

We don't often hear the word "commitment" these days. More familiar are we with trendy terms extolling "freedom," "choice," "significant others," "relationships" ("meaningful," of course), and "having it our way." Honoring a marriage vow for life would hardly fit these contemporary by-words.

Robert Louis Stevenson once remarked, "Marriage is one long conversation chequered by disputes." If so, then in all truth, my parents' marriage had more disputes than conversations. All the more cause for celebration, I say!

My folks came from a breed that believed you stayed married because you said you would and your faith would sustain you through any obstacle. And obstacles mom and dad certainly did have.

My parents persevered through a depression, one major war, and another war that took, for a time, their youngest son. They hung tough through bouts of workaholism, alcoholism, mental illness, a parade of live-in friends and relatives needing bed and board during wartime, and a dependent mother followed by a sickly father. Added to this was the adoption of three children which certainly must have aided in the grey hair, sleepless nights, and vanished dreams. Yet, they have never ceased telling us that our coming was one of the happiest events in their married lives.

Now that's commitment.

Not to tarnish their good names, nor discredit their fifty-plus-year record, but to paint a scene of "happily ever after" would do them a disservice. After all, anyone can make it through a fairyland, Disneyland, or Christmas. It takes real courage to continue when there are more obstacles than avenues. It takes faith to continue when you don't always "feel like it." And it takes a love that many of us will never know, to give and to care for another for a lifetime because you vowed you always would. That's commitment. Differences, more than similarities, were the mark of my parents' relationship.

Dad is a quick-tempered, chauvinistic Italian whose lifestyle was "all work and no play." His one mode of relaxation, hobby farming, even required work. Mom is German and a perfectionist devoted to home and family, but she once caused a memorable marital explosion by taking dancing lessons with a girlfriend "just for fun." Dad was sure she had lost her mind.

Dad has lived his entire life in the same section of Northeast Minneapolis. He is non-political, a stubborn homebody, hating change, disrupted schedules, shopping, or vacations away from home. Mom, on the other hand, is a transplant from Iowa. She loves American politics, travel, and change for the sake of change. She's been to the West, Southwest, and East coasts, as well as to Europe and the Holy Land — while dad stays home and goes to the farm. The few trips she has managed to coax dad on have been disastrous. On each, she was sick of home and he was homesick. She called it a holiday. He thought it horrible.

Mom has always loved picnics, Sunday drives around Lake Harriet, and shopping (with charge cards) at downtown's finest. Dad detests "paying on time," thinks most things can be bought at K Mart, and his idea of recreation is to stand, by the hour, with beer in hand, in front of the feed trough watching his pigs wrestle for their dinner.

I'm convinced that mom and dad made it to their Golden Anniversary and beyond because, in spite of the obstacles and differences, their faith and value systems were fundamentally one. A good lesson to our young seek-

93

ing a lifetime partner. There can be no "till death do us part" if only one spouse believes it.

In today's world we know that probably one in every three to four marriages will end in divorce. Most splits occur before the fifth year of marriage. The blame lies not entirely with the couple, however, but with a narcissistic society that promotes abandonment of vows that seem no longer continually pleasurable or convenient to fulfill. The media, permissive peers, a "Me" generation, and, in some cases, confused clerics, advise couples encountering stormy seas to "jump ship" for smoother sailing. In my folks' time, the rule was, "Man the battle stations and full speed ahead!" Divorce was not an option. Death was the only "out."

At a recent family wedding, one of my Italian uncles leaned over to talk to me during the reception. His words seem to summarize the generational gap we live in, as he commented on the number of nieces and nephews already divorced. "I'm sure glad I'm older and didn't marry during your generation. I never would have made it. In fact, most of us wouldn't have. There's just too much temptation now to throw in the towel, and look what I would have missed," he said, as he affectionately looked at his wife, children, and grandchildren seated around him. They, like my parents, had had their marital "disputes" (one, serious enough to warrant a two-year separation). But for them, "La Familia" was worth the struggle.

Unfortunately, many in my era do not have the fortitude, faith, or perhaps the freedom, to pledge such long-term commitment to any other person, cause, or ideal. In fact, the most frequent promise today, is to "be good to yourself."

This generation seeks a life guaranteed free from pain, discomfort, boredom, or unhappiness. Other human beings become commodities in an endless "pursuit of happiness." Marriage as a lifetime commitment is no longer a given.

Even the "family" section of our newspaper has been renamed "Variety" — more aptly portraying the smorgasbord of living arrangements touted as equal to, if not better, than the once-sacrosanct traditional marriage. We read of pre-nuptial contracts, legal agreements and renewable or revocable pledges in place of ". . . till death do us part."

For the bored or adventuresome, there is "open marriage" and what was once the avenue of last resort — the unavoidable, the worst of all worlds — DIVORCE — has become attractive, respectable, and even commendable. By law, we have decreed divorce to be "no fault" — the goal seeming to be a pain-free, if not downright friendly, parting of the ways.

Of course, there are those marriages in which divorce is the only or ultimate solution. Commitment takes two. A pledge to be faithful for a lifetime must be freely given and upheld by both individuals.

When one physically or psychologically abandons such a promise, the other is left with the void. No one can cling to a void. To those left in the wake of such abandonment, we must offer our love and support. At such times, they need family and friends more than ever. But their pain, however, is trivialized by a society which categorizes such a status as a desirable vocation.

President James Garfield once made the comment that "the sanctity of marriage and the family relation make the cornerstone of our American society and civilization." Honore de Balzac, the French novelist, amplified this concept by observing, "When a man and woman are married, their romance ceases and their history commences."

In my parents' case, their romance certainly did not cease — though it was not always obvious to those in their company. What became apparent was the legacy they established. Because of them, and so many like them who made no headlines and gathered neither fortune nor fame, their children and grandchildren inherited an immeasurable trust. They taught us commitment. They did not preach their faithfulness, nor harp on values or standards. They simply lived them.

Ah, to have the inner stuff of that generation before us. They so naively pledged and plunged into an unknown sea of conjugal commitment. For them, marriage was a forever thing.

# Chapter 15

# Bonds And Roots

I recently drove my folks to Hudson, Wisconsin (once known as "Little Italy") where more than two hundred relatives gathered to celebrate a distant member's eightieth birthday. During the drive from Minneapolis, mom spoke of her high blood pressure, stiff joints, and arthritic knees. Dad relived "the last time we went to Hudson," reciting the names of those loved ones who had since died, reminding us at intervals that it's "tough to get old."

When we arrived, the small-town VFW hall was bursting with music, dancing, and a crowd of hand-waving, cheek-pinching Italian mamas and papas.

As I watched my folks talk to cousins, nieces, nephews, aunts, and uncles, it seemed as if troubles appeared manageable, sorrow bearable, and age took a leap backward. Ten minutes after our arrival, mom and dad were joking with relatives about bygone days, and shared moments of joy. The warm eyes, gladdened hearts, and fond embraces easily erased the added wrinkles, and padded waistlines. My mother, a transplanted German from Oelwein, Iowa, blended with dad's Italian kin as if serving pasta and canning hot green peppers was her native birthright. The only give-away is her name and Lucille Ball-red hair.

"Wilma, you never seem to age. You barely have a wrinkle, and you're just as pretty as ever."

"Aw Luigi, you old flirt, you always say such nice things. You know I'm getting old. . . ," my mom, who is in her mid seventies, laughingly retorted — looking more youthful and light-hearted as she spoke.

A reunion is an invitation to let nostalgia take over, to leave behind the work-a-day world of stress, the impersonal universe of high-tech pressures. No wonder people flock to such rendezvous!

Large family gatherings bring back the sweet and not-so-sweet memories that remind us of who we were and why we are — those innocent childhoods and perhaps not-so-innocent adolescent antics. It's a time to remember, reminisce, recall, and relive.

Family members are the people you don't have to work to impress. You can be yourself. There's no test to pass, no fee to belong. You have a right to be included simply because you are.

In family life, there's little room for superficiality, especially phoniness, arrogance, or a "better-than-thou" attitude. So who's impressed? These are the people who know you best. After all, you're related and they knew you "when. . . ."

On another side of the family, my husband's brother-in-law travels from Washington State to North Dakota every other year for what has become a family reunion of over two hundred fifty relatives. It's a party he refuses to miss.

My friend Anne goes home to Detroit each Christmas to be with her Serbian relatives. When her mother, the matriarch of the clan, died during the year, they still came together. "She was our reason for going home," Anne said. "Yet now more than before we want to get together, so we don't lose touch."

For those who have no family, our pastor suggests they surround themselves with friends and a faith community which offers meaning and a sense of belonging. As Father says, "It's very important we take time out to have a little party, to celebrate with others, and enjoy life."

It is a demographic fact that America is experiencing the most mobile, "disconnected" generation ever.

Henry, an acquaintance of ours, is a case in point. He uprooted his wife and children and took them away from Minnesota friends, family, and familiarity for one reason: the promise of more money (read comfort level) in Oklahoma. So it was goodbye hometown. Goodbye grandma and grandpa, brothers, and sisters. Goodbye friends, neighbors, and family ties. And hello Oklahoma and hello money. Only Henry will be able to measure if the profit was worth the loss.

Today, children often work and raise their children far from the grandparents whose lives may have to revolve around some antiseptic retirement community. Even holidays that were once exclusively reserved for family are now used by some as mini-vacation opportunities, with little regard for the traditions, custom, or kin left behind. We may be nearing an era when Disneyland, Epcot Center, and Sea World take precedence over grandma and grandpa.

And yet paradoxically, this mobile age has brought with it a fixation on roots and bonds, even if in fleeting, small doses. More and more, we read and hear about giant family reunions when individuals, who bear little more than a last name in common, will eagerly fly across the continent to be one of the tribe. They'll sleep in cabins, tents, trailers, and spare rooms, all for the luxury of congregating with others who claim kinship and mutual ancestry. There's not much time for in-depth interaction, mind you — just a few days off for fun and nostalgia.

We have the highly mobile strivers who reject family homestead and heritage for adventure and the unknown, and who seem to hunger for the very bonds and ties that they so easily broke. A reunion, wedding, birthday, anniversary, or even a funeral, can for a brief moment restore the sense of identity and bearings lost when family ties are broken.

Perhaps it is not until the ties are broken that many people realize how much they meant.

In the end, the kids of this generation may be the most deprived of all. Few have experienced the thrill of a big family celebration or know, except in a more, formal and planned setting, their great Uncle Joe, Aunt Betty, or for that matter, even grandma and grandpa.

With today's talk of "unwanted children" and abortion promoted as choice, I've come to realize that I'm one of the most fortunate of individuals to so freely celebrate the gift of this large Italian family from whence I came, with all its interwoven roots, heritage, bonds, and sibling ties. After all, I was adopted and have no real "blood lines" with anyone in my immediate world. Adopted and "twice loved," as the saying goes — once by a mother who selflessly gave me life and a future, and again by a family that taught me how to love and gave me roots and a sense of belonging — as if there had been a gaping void without me.

*(The above was previously published in Newsweek 8/21/89)*

*Chapter 16*

# The Goodness Of Extended Family

I feel sorry for the kids of today who may never know the experience of EXTENDED family. In the 40s, 50s, and 60s we had no VCRs, ear-phoned radios, or video centers, but as I reflect back, I believe my cousins and I, and many like us, were far richer than the children of today. We had grandma and grandpa very much in our lives.

Today's age demands a more mobile society. It's a rare family in this era who can boast of parents and grandparents within walking or (short) driving distance. With the virtual demise of family-farm communities, and the advent of home-to-work distance commuting, it's hard enough for husband and wife to see each other seven days of every week.

In fact, some put their marriage on hold until the weekend, when they can fly or drive back to their mate. Lost in the shuffle are the children of this "new age" life-style, and their grandparents and extended family members who must settle for an all-too-infrequent (not to mention SHORT and costly) visit.

Some people relocate for the fun, adventure, and newness of change. Most, however, do so because their type of employment REQUIRES the move.

Without question, the individuals who suffer their own kind of pain are those children, grandparents, and extended family members who are prevented from fully sharing in one another's lives because of divorce.

Certainly, those who remember well their own childhood and the vivid impressions of warmth and love created by grandma and grandpa or that favored aunt or uncle, would wish to provide the same for their own youngsters.

In their heart-of-hearts, they realize that the highly programmed and fleeting trips home (arranged mostly around weddings, funerals, and holidays) could hardly give their young that same involved and leisurely time to REALLY get to know those loved ones and the sensations of touch, smell and taste that come from rocking-chair storytimes, special cookies and treats, casual walks or hours passed with a beloved grandparent.

Some years back, my husband, John, and I made the purposeful decision to make our home state our permanent residence. In order to keep this resolve, John passed up more than one lucrative out-of-town job offer. Yet, never for a minute have we regretted it.

We live within driving distance of both of our parents. Although our relationship with our parents is far from perfect, we have come to believe there is a certain sense of security, continuity, and normalcy that is a blessing and a gift to our lives. Whether it is a crisis, death, or a special event, it takes on even more meaning for children when close relatives, most especially grandparents, are present.

As for memories: In our kids' minds, nothing is better than a visit at grandma's house. After all, who else has such marvelous old jewelry (even the button drawer is fun!), dress-up clothes, and toys from the 40s and 50s? And who, but a grandma, will listen (by the hour) to a little one's tale or an exuberant teen talk about that "awesome" date or night at the prom?

Each grandma and grandpa, we believe, has left a distinct never-to-be-forgotten mark on our children, including John's dad who never lived long enough to see more than our first two children. And yet, our Tim and Michael, and Joseph in particular, are spittin' images of this once robust, happy-faced Polish giant of a man.

John's mom (Grandma K) who died a few months after Joseph, our youngest child's, first birthday, was known as the "little Grandma." Every time we'd tell her we were adding another to our crew, she would throw up her hands and exclaim, "You guys are really crazy!"

But guess who was there to welcome this new little someone the minute he or she was in our arms — Yep, Grandma Kuharski.

She was the practical giver who remembered the needed pajamas, underwear, play clothes, and favorite food or treat that lit up a birthday kid's eyes. In the winter months, she would sometimes "take two at a time" for an overnight. So special were these times to our children that each one knew when his turn was next. In the summer, it was at Grandma K's cabin that we vacationed, and it's because of her that our children know how to bait a hook (her patience bordered on heroic!), repair a broken line, clean a fish, and play Canasta, Hearts, Go-To-The-Dump, and whatever else they could con her into. She never once complained about us taking over her two-bedroom hideaway — nor about her flattened grass, smudged walls and door handles, smeared windows, and the "sand-everywhere" floor. What a jewel this "little Grandma" was and what an untold loss to us, when she died.

By contrast, my mom is known as the "one that wears lipstick and drives a car." Being a bit taller and plumper than John's mom, she is called "Big Grandma."

Mom just loves to see our children "look special," and realizing the budget we must live by, it is she who sees to it the girls have that frilly dress and the boys new pants or a shirt at Christmas time — with bonnets for the little ones at Easter — and a permanent wave (given by grandma) for any of us who need "just a little curl around the face." Nothing's more exciting than piling in the car to go on a shopping spree (which also means "lunch out") with "Big Grandma." Grandma makes each one of our brood feel loved and "priceless." When they are with her, they really do feel special, because of the way she listens to them and encourages their accomplishments.

My dad holds his place of honor and is remembered most for his gift "to each one" of a new dollar on special occasions, and for the family drives and picnics we've shared on his hobby farm. As city kids, my boys especially cherished their Saturdays on the farm: shoveling manure, gathering eggs, and bailing hay.

He's not a man of eloquent words, nor gushy emotion. Peppery phrases and no-nonsense dialogue is more his style. He tells it like *he* sees it.

When Tony (age 18) recently showed up at Grandpa's sporting a silver earring hanging from one ear, Grandpa minced few words in telling Tony what he thought of it. "He told me not to come over again looking like that," said Tony. "That's okay. I told him I was there to mow his lawn even if he doesn't like my new look. I know he loves me no matter what he says."

Pity the couples who can't afford the luxury that we've had of living near extended family.

I often wonder just who do others turn to when they have no such extended family member close by? What do they do when those large or little instances arise and there's no one who knows them well to turn to for advice, consolation, satisfaction, or encouragement?

Of course, we've experienced our share of disappointment, heartache, and tension. But is there any family that is free of friction, disharmony, interruptions, or interference? I doubt it. It's times such as these when the meaning of family can be more bitter than sweet, and yet, it has been our experience that just such occasions can offer us the greatest opportunities to grow in love and faith.

After all, it's easy to write a check to feed the hungry in far-off India, to work in the soup line, to stack shelves for the homeless in the inner city, or to run a pledge drive for charity. The true test of our worth may come in being kind, open, and forgiving to members of our own family.

The Fourth Commandment does more than compel us to "Honor Thy Father and Mother," it sets a standard of care and concern. To those children who offer love and respect to their parents, even when faced with great obstacles (such as distance, differences, or illness (including senility, alcoholism, or incapacity) we can be assured that God is never outdone in generosity. Whatsoever we give will be returned "a hundred fold."

Proverbs 13:22 tells us: "The good man leaves an inheritance to his children's children." What greater inheritance could we leave our young than the intangible wealth that comes from the knowledge, companionship, and love of grandparents and relatives?

For those who have the opportunity to offer their young a life involved with a loving extended family, and most importantly a grandparent, time is of the essence and the future so fleeting. Better grab that chance while you can. We did and we've found that even after death, the benefits and blessings remain with us.

# Chapter 17

# Taking Toddlers To Church

There were many a time, during the course of our parenting years, when attending Sunday Mass with our children seemed more burden than blessing. While we never gave in to the temptation to go in split shifts, or to skip Mass altogether, we certainly had our periods of frustration and aggravation. Short of going to church in rotation, hiring a sitter, or putting the kids in a nursery, there is a way to make Sunday attendance a family affair. Here are some practical tips we've learned that may help you over the challenging time of taking toddlers to church.

First of all we must remember:

**\* Children need to pray and worship, too.** Children belong in Church where they can imitate their parents and other members of the congregation. An acquaintance of ours warned friends not to fall into the trap they set for themselves when their youngsters were small. The parents began a weekly routine of dropping the children at grandma's house. The two boys were treated to pancakes and grandma, while mom and dad went to Church.

As the youngsters grew older, the parents decided it was time they begin attending church. It was quite an ordeal, however, to replace pancakes and grandma with silence, reverence, and discipline.

It would have been far better for the boys if they had learned as toddlers that going to church was a family activity, pleasing to God, to others, and eventually to themselves. A visit with grandma could be reserved for after church.

Early training in the formation of religious traditions and practices is like planting seeds of faith that will take root and grow along with the child. In fact, most Catholics who confess to a period of non-practice in their faith commitment, say it was the good memory of their early and sound religious upbringing that coaxed their eventual return to the Church.

 * **Remember that going to church on Sunday gives glory to God and keeps His commandments.** Taking toddlers to church is the best example parents can give to their young. Of course, perhaps there will always be Sundays when parents, because of crying infants, antsy toddlers, or family hassle, don't FEEL much like that "Mystical Body of Christ." Yet, these are just such times that God will bless us most for our efforts and faithful witness.

 The Holy Father, Pope John Paul II, teaches that "prayer constitutes an essential part of christian life." It is an expression of the family's union with Christ. It also builds and nourishes that union. And, he says, "Family prayer will die without the sacramental ministry of the universal Church, especially the sacraments of Penance and the Holy Eucharist."

 To Catholics, the Mass, and reception of the Holy Eucharist, is Christ's continual gift to us, His people. There is no form of worship or prayer that equals the power and the grace to be received.

 Christians of ALL faiths, give glory to God, and nourish their children's faith, (regardless of the ruckus) each time they give public worship to God.

### BEFORE CHURCH:
 * **Be prepared for baby's needs.** When you take an infant to church, bring bottles, pacifier, diapers, and a bib. People would much rather see a child enjoy his/her dinner than hear the baby crying for it. For the nursing mom, wear skirts with a top that can be easily adjusted to nursing. Seek a chair in the back of the church or in a separate room if feeding time is a noticeable disruption.

 Most nursing mothers have so mastered the art of discretion in their nursing methods that such an event goes

107

virtually unnoticed by others. One mother said, "When I had my first child and was nursing, I purposely went to Saturday evening Mass or attended a separate service from my husband, in order to avoid the possibility of having a waking or crying baby eager to nurse. When our second child came along, Jack and I dreaded the thought of the months of going to church separately, so we resolved to try to take the children and go together. At first, when the baby needed to nurse I went to the basement. Later, I got a bit braver and sat in a chair off to the side or back of church. I soon realized that the people around me, no matter where I sat, were completely unaware that this was baby's feeding time. They were engrossed in their own thoughts and prayers. All that anxiety about nursing in public was for nought."

For the restless infant or small toddler, a selection of small toys (forget the rattles and noisemakers) are appropriate time-passers. It helps if these are not the same toys he or she sees and plays with every day. One mother kept a small toy collection in her diaper bag just for those church, doctor's office waits, or other occasions from home.

**\* Include your children in your prayer intentions.** Even young preschoolers will better understand why you pray and what specific things you pray for, if they learn to share in the Mass and prayer intentions of their parents.

We formed the early habit of telling our children, before going to Mass or saying the evening Rosary, for whom or what we were praying.

For instance, John might start the ball rolling by saying, "Today mom and dad want to offer this up for Mr. Johnson who is in the hospital and very sick, and also in thanksgiving for the wonderful family reunion we had at grandma and grandpa's house last week. Do you have any other intentions you would like to add?"

In this way, youngsters, early on, begin to form a sense of prayer for reasons of praise, thanksgiving, petition, and contrition.

It took very little prompting before the kids' prayer petitions outnumbered ours. In fact, we are often amazed at the "grownup" attitude some of our little ones have in their prayer reflections.

The practice of encouraging children to think of certain people or issues to pray for gives special meaning to prayer and Sunday Mass and heightens the importance of each Mass or prayer.

As parents, we must eagerly encourage our young to believe that NO prayer is too small, and no person too young to get God's attention and help. In fact, our Heavenly Father, who calls us to a "child-like faith" may find a youngster's prayer the most powerful and irresistible of all.

"I know Jesus will help us because we always ask Him when we pray," as our Kari, then six, so trustingly stated.

* **Wear your Sunday best.** A youngster can tell the importance of an event by the way others look and dress. Our rule of thumb is: Sunday clothes don't have to be expensive or fancy — just different and somewhat fussier than the usual "everyday apparel." A special dress, suit, coat, shoes, or hat, is not only fun for a child but the specialness of the clothes reminds him or her that visiting God is something for which we all dress nice. Going to church becomes an anticipated occasion and the special clothing, a sign of respect for others and reverence for God. *(This is an area where a grandparent, godparents, or a caring aunt or uncle might add a helping hand.)*

I frankly admit, that during some difficult times in the past, while trying to stay within our family budget, I got out of the habit of buying new outfits for Easter and Christmas. One year my mother came over a few weeks before Easter, and loaded our youngest girls (Mary, Angela, and Kari) in the car to go shopping for Easter bonnets. The girls came home delighted after the lunch and fun shopping spree with grandma and were thrilled with their new hats. On Easter morning we never saw three more eager children get dressed for church, and the glow lasted throughout the whole summer.

* **Be sure pre-schoolers are ready.** Children should

have a good breakfast and ALWAYS go to the bathroom just before leaving home. Some youngsters fuss simply because they are hungry. While adults can usually postpone a morning meal or coffee and roll till later, children need to eat breakfast. Their built-in alarms often urge them toward lunch long before their folks feel such hunger pangs.

As for the bathroom, DON'T take chances. It's easier and SAFER to take preschoolers out during the service than to take the risk of underestimating their need. Some children truly can't wait one more minute, and no one wants to meet the new pastor over a mop.

* **Bring children's books.** There are wonderful booklets on faith and the meaning of the Mass and Eucharist especially designed for children. These usually contain colorful pictures and are written in a language easily understood. Be sure your child has a special prayer book and save it for church use only, so the child will not grow tired of the pictures and story. Even better, have several selections and rotate their use.

* **Things to avoid.** Try to discourage the children from bringing large dolls, trucks, or food and candy that is sticky and messy — not only for your sake, but out of respect for the people who will sit in the pew for the next Mass. People resent sitting in pews that bear the gummy remains of a child's sucker or chewing gum. Also, the sight of another child eating in Church has set off many a chain reaction from other toddlers screaming, "I want some, too."

Eating snacks in church is distracting and diminishes the reverence due a place of worship. For one hour a week a child can learn to do without food and treats. In fact, the offering of sweets to persuade an unruly youngster, is counterproductive as it may only serve to reinforce disruptive or bad behavior.

### AT CHURCH:
* **Sit up front.** Through trial and error — and I do mean "trial and error" — we've learned that a toddler or young child always behaves better if he or she has a front row seat.

Put yourself in your child's place. With the limited eye level a preschooler has, imagine yourself seated behind rows of parishioners. The priest and altar are far up front, and a youngster can hardly be expected to pay attention if his or her vision is blocked by the backs of others.

Many parents have been pleasantly surprised to see their previously squirming child transformed to a quiet, attentive observer — all because they had changed their seating habits and the youngsters could see what was going on.

Our neighbors Paul and Pat told of the change in their son when they moved to the front. "Every Sunday was a 'Pick-me-up,' 'Hold me,' 'Put-me-down,' match of the wills with Tommy (eighteen months) as we attempted to keep him still and prevent him from crawling under and around the pews. Paul and I took turns holding him, promising, threatening, and scolding. We didn't dare move up front. Yet after finally trying it 'just once' we couldn't believe it!

"Tommy was better than he'd ever been and each week his behavior improved. We never thought he could sit so still. He is far more content now that he can watch and listen to what's going on around him."

**\* Support from clergy and community.** Many a young couple is thankful when pastor and congregation openly encourage the presence of small children. While some churches have nurseries or insist that parents stay in the "crying room" with their children, it is to those who utter, "Suffer the little ones to come unto me" that there awaits a greater reward.

This is not to suggest that parishioners be subjected to rages, continued outbursts, or temper tantrums. On the contrary, every parent must recognize there are days when no amount of coaxing or preparation will ward off unruliness. When those moments occur it is time to remove the child and know in your heart that the Lord will honor your intention.

Don't worry about the occasions when you "don't get anything out of the service." God will bless you for trying, and for the image you create for your child and surrounding community who observe you, and He will see the importance of faith in your life.

Most of our crew did reasonably well at Sunday liturgy, yet over the years we did experience our share of "exceptions." When those times occurred, stashing our "disrupter" in the nursery was a salvation to our central nervous systems!

* **Expect good behavior.** Children need to learn early, that there are some occasions during which they must refrain from talk or play. This teaching is the beginning of good self-discipline. Even young toddlers are eager to please and to copy the actions of their loved ones. It doesn't take too much effort on a parent's part before a child, from observation, will begin to show a more reserved behavior.

Of course, there are times when the only recourse left to a mom and dad with a fussy or crying child is to leave the pew. In that regard, we discovered that instead of leaving church altogether, sometimes just the motion of moving to the back vestibule and the change of scenery stopped the fussy behavior and got us through the remainder of Mass.

* **Be sure to praise your child for good behavior.** Compliment them for good behavior just as you would chastise them for bad behavior. Children love to feel appreciated, noticed, and praised for their actions. Most youngsters are only too eager to repeat the same good deeds or behavior that won them the praise and attention the first time.

* **Insist that your child try, but don't expect perfection.** Be patient yet persistent. Children do outgrow disruptive behavior. Most "been there" parents suggest that it takes a few weeks or months for a youngster to adjust to an "in-church" atmosphere.

* **Encourage your child to participate.** Children like to feel a part of things and they should be given an active role in the goings on at Church.

We take advantage of special opportunities when our kids can participate. A family Baptism, holding a candle at the Easter Vigil service, or lighting an occasional vigil light, brings a sense of reverence and makes children feel an integral part of worship.

If your parish has a weekly food drive or collection, encourage your son or daughter to offer the donated items as your family representative. The influence of sacramentals (Holy Water, blessed candles, and palms) should not be ignored. We put up a small Holy Water font and were really surprised at how much it meant to the children and how reverently they treated it. On Palm Sunday, we let our children carry the palms home and choose the place in our home where they remain throughout the year. Even small kids love taking an active part.

Children will participate and sing at Church with little prompting. Most youngsters love music and even if your child is too small to read, he or she can enjoy the singing. You might consider buying a record of religious music.

 * **Intend to pray yourself.** Make a deliberate intention and sincere effort to pray while at the Sunday liturgy. This may seem rather elementary and yet, in the words of a Minneapolis pastor, "An effort to pray is very important and CAN be overlooked by young parents who have struggled to dress and feed their children and make sure all get to church on time. They can become so preoccupied with trying to make the hour go well and without disturbance for the priest and people around them, they forget to truly intend to pray, to converse with Jesus."

The *mere* intention to pray is a devout prayer and should be a great source of strength to parents when Sunday or daily distractions frustrate our spiritual efforts.

In fact, the words of St. Augustine can be especially encouraging to parents of a young and active family. He said, "There is another sort of prayer, namely desire, and that prayer is uninterrupted. Whatever you are doing, if you are desiring the Sabbath, you are praying incessantly even without words" (*A Doorway to Silence*, Robert Llewelyn, "St. Augustine and unceasing prayer," p. 47).

His thoughts apply, not just for Sunday Mass, but all through our life effort to pray and become closer to God.

My Aunt Dolores, who speaks from experience after raising six children, said a morning prayer was her best assurance that her whole day was an offering to God. "I learned to begin each day, including Sunday, by saying The Morning Offering, and it was this prayer intention to offer my daily happenings that often got me through the most hectic of times and made me feel God saw all of it as my own little prayer to Him."

St. Therese of Lisieux ("The Little Flower"), aptly called the "greatest saint of modern times," lived as a cloistered Carmelite nun and died an agonizing death at the age of twenty-four. She served her community as a laundress, offering her daily work and sufferings for the honor and glory of God — calling it her "Little Way" for Christ. This marked her a saint to be emulated by all.

So often mothers and fathers dismiss their daily tasks and chores as responsibilities done by rote with no meaningful goodness. The assumption is that unless some great visible act of charity has been performed, the day-to-day efforts appear quite meaningless. St. Therese is but one among a host of great saints who proved the opposite to be true. It is important for those who dedicate themselves to serving others through family life, (doing laundry, dishes, homemaking, car repair, bill balancing, etc.) to understand that even the most grand charitable acts, if done for no eternal worth or purpose, does not compare with the most insignificant of deeds if done out of love of God.

* **Make the Lord's Day special.** Reserve your fun sprees like visits to family, friends, or outings to the zoo, etc., for the Lord's Day. This way the whole day is one your child looks forward to with anticipation. Most couples have seen the importance of getting to know their pastor and parish staff, and becoming active in church activities. Children will identify and become more comfortable with surroundings and people they see on a frequent basis. One father told of his child's delight at seeing Father Smith on the altar — having recognized him as the one who had been present at a previous family function.

**\* Attend church together as a family.** If at all possible, make Sunday a truly "family affair" by going to church together. This self-imposed "unity" may involve more effort than taking turns, or going in shifts, but the benefits will almost always outweigh the hassle.

Most certainly, there are situations, such as when a new baby arrives or special events or weekend employment, that conflict with church attendance as a family.

Sunday should be viewed as "The Lord's Day," however, and should be reserved as a time to pray and worship together — the one day during a busy week, when friends, hobbies, or outside interests take a back seat to family.

**\* Don't let your youngsters form the habit of going to church alone or with a group of friends.** Once again, allowances must always be made for special events, conflicting schedules in the family, or because of outside employment, when insisting on family attendance together at church.

Jack Quesnell, an internationally known author (*Beyond Your Wedding Day*), and marriage and family counselor says, "In my practice I have found that for the most part, the words of Father Peyton are so true: 'The family that prays together — stays together.' "

**\* One last thought.** We cannot expect that the presence of babies and small children in Church is going to produce an austere setting, no matter how much preparation and prayer. Assuredly, there will always be an occasional cry or outburst.

On the other hand, we live in an era in which millions of youngsters are victims of abuse, abandonment, and abortion. Perhaps we should view the occasional or uncontrolled cry of children in our midst, as a gentle and subtle reminder to pray for those less fortunate who have no opportunity to offer their own "joyful noise to the Lord."

# Chapter 18

# Controlling The Tube
# Before It Controls Us

When it comes to today's television programs, this is one family that has "tuned out" and "turned off." We have joined the ranks of millions of other Christians who carefully censor and control the television programming allowed in their home.

It hit home one day when I came home after attending a meeting at church. When I walked in, my children were engrossed in a Sunday evening thirty-minute sitcom. I was just in time to see a pretty young girl snuggle up to her bashful pursuer and ask, "Would you like to kiss me? Would you like to rip off all my clothes and have sex with me?"

The TV response was five seconds of canned laughter at which my younger children looked on in confusion. This, on prime time, is hardly a notion parents want embedded in their children's minds.

How far we've wandered from the wholesome family entertainment once offered during prime time. And how far too, from the initial concept that TV was an instrument of enjoyment, a virtual "must," for every American home.

We should no longer ignore the fact that endless hours of TV watching not only stifles youngsters' curious and creative minds, but the programs offered, in many respects, are neither educational, entertaining, or appropriate for Christian families.

Dr. Sidney Hook, a respected American philosopher, claims that the use of tranquilizers is a reflection on the power of television. "In part I blame the media, especially television, for this whole problem (of alcohol and chemical abuse). People have been taught it is not necessary to experience any more. . . . They have adopted a passive mode of living. They let all the outside forces, such as television do it for them."

Many others working in the drug abuse field agree. Dr. Anthony Kales, chairman of the Department of Psychiatry at Pennsylvania State University, believes television advertising has a tremendous impact on the young. He believes "it encourages the widespread use of drugs for what usually are responses to normal frustrations of life." Youngsters, he said, need to develop a proper frustration tolerance through role modeling of adults who "can withstand the stresses and anxieties in everyday life. But in the drug/pain TV advertisements, adults are depicted as very quick to take medication to relieve even the most minimal level of anxiety, sleeplessness, or pain. The young viewer is provided an extremely negative role model. . . ." Dr. Kales believes it is a very small step to extend this concept of immediate self-medication of over-the-counter drugs to immediate mood alteration with drugs of abuse."

English novelist Edward George Bulwer contends, "Children and genius have the same master organ in common — inquisitiveness." In the face of modern at-home videos, cable, twenty-four-hour broadcasting, and drop-in video establishments, what American youngster has a chance to pursue a creative inquisitiveness unless a line of restraint is drawn?

My husband and I realized that our Christian values would corrode from under us unless we enforced some strict limitations.

We chose the beginning of Lent to launch our campaign to limit the family's TV viewing. The rule for the six weeks of Lent was: No television, except news shows and specials.

Our decision to "limit" was not greeted without opposition. However, it required everyone, including my husband and I, to shed some old habits.

Like most parents today, we grew up with television, making it more difficult to censor our own children's viewing.

Were there periods of backsliding? You bet! Keep in mind we have a houseful of youngsters ranging in age from infants to late teens who were accustomed to watching unlimited television every evening. Their reaction to our family Lenten offering was typical of normal, healthy kids. They were horrified.

They tried, on more than one occasion, to bend the rules for "exceptions." We heard everything from, "But this is such a good show," to "My teacher told us to watch it," and more commonly, "There's nothing else to do."

One son predicted that he and his sisters and brothers would "just end up fighting more" if the TV was curtailed. In fact, the pining and whining for the tube is not exclusive to little ones. Half the young people at our house are teens. They are hardworking, fun-loving kids. They earn their own way through paper routes and part-time jobs and have little time — or so we thought — to spend hours in front of the set. Yet, when we instituted "no TV during Lent except news shows and specials," one daughter pleaded exception because she is over eighteen and "watches so little TV." Another said, "It relaxes me after a hard day at school and work." Our seventeen-year-old son claimed, "TV's the ONLY enjoyment I get out of life." Hmmmmm!

The more they protested, the more we realized how much we all needed a more permanent break from the tube. Lent was a good beginning, helping us to wean ourselves — in "cold turkey" fashion — and to establish some rules and guides for the rest of the year.

To make our Lenten withdrawal as painless as possible we initially did more things with the kids. We went for walks, played card and board games, helped them select books at the library, and occasionally watched home movies as a family.

There was little need to worry about becoming television's permanent replacement or having to create daily activities for them, however. Once the children got used to the free time they had gained, their desire to be entertained quickly diminished as they began to create their own entertainment. Meanwhile, we found it a wonderful chance to capture some tender and fun moments that we would otherwise have missed had we or they been passively engrossed in television watching.

Today, television viewing is limited to the evening (after dinner) hours (one to two in the winter months and one, or none, in the summer), with news shows or specials as the exceptions.

When springtime comes, we institute the "Sunshine Law" rejecting even the most popular shows in favor of the backyard swingset, basketball hoop, a walk around the block, or a good novel. (We Midwesterners who for the most part, spend winter months indoors should not have to be coaxed off the couch and away from the tube come sunshine and warm weather.)

Of course, along with curtailing the hours of viewing, we recognized the need to control the content of the television programs our children watch as well. Up until then, I think our kids would have watched an old 1950s style black and white test pattern, as long as they thought something else would eventually come after. They had formed such a habit of turning it on at the same time each evening, there was little regard for what they were tuning in.

We now insist that they ask permission before using the television. When we first began restricting television, our conversations went something like this:

> "Dad, can we watch TV?" Kari asked.
> "Sure," dad responded. "What's on?"
> "I don't know," said flustered Kari.
> "Well, you can't watch just anything. Unless you can tell me what program you want to see, and it's one we know to be a decent show, you can't turn the set on."

The kids would race for the newspaper to check the listings. Oftentimes, they didn't bother coming back to appeal their case. They knew, sometimes more than we, that "nothing's on that's any good."

The practice of asking first reminds youngsters that the television set belongs to the parents, not the children, and is a privilege not to be abused. Requiring children to ask for permission to watch television also prevents them from watching out of boredom, with no thought as to a program's content or worth. In addition, asking kept us at the controls and offered them the opportunity to become selective in the shows they chose to watch.

It goes without saying that we don't permit ANY child to watch a program or video that we believe is distasteful, vulgar, or objectionable. We let our young know that parents have automatic veto power.

We have explained to our kids that "as Christian parents we not only have the right but a *moral obligation* to limit their viewing habits, especially if we feel something is tasteless, offensive, or detrimental to their development."

In another vein, many a busy mom has been tempted to use the tube as a babysitter or pacifier to keep rowdy or rambunctious kids in control. I know from firsthand experience. Two of my boys were hyperactive run-abouts whose motors never seemed to wear down. However, even the most boisterous youngsters respond positively when encouraged to play constructively. In fact, many youngsters weaned from TV are LESS frenzied than those temporarily tranquilized. Patience, praise, and prayer were my keys to success. I also kept (on top of the refrigerator and doled out accordingly), a $2.00 paint set, a container of old-fashioned modeling clay, and a finger paint set (with old paintshirts and tablecloths) for those rainy or harried days when I just "had to get something done" and my Michael (age four) and Dominic (age three) were determined to undo everything I did.

Watching good programs on television can be a unifying experience. If watched together, as a family, television can educate, stimulate, and promote discussion between parents and children. This is program-viewing at its finest.

Conversely, if rules are not established it can also cause division and stifle family unity. At our house we do not allow television in our children's rooms, nor do we allow our young adults to have a set of their own, even if they can afford to buy one. We tell them we love them enough to say, "No." The more isolated individual family members become, the easier it is to build walls. The more children learn to consider, compromise, and bend to the wishes of others, the less self-centered they will be.

After the initial stage of withdrawal, grumbling, and boredom, our children became preoccupied with their new library books, art projects, and creative play. They stopped checking the paper "to see what's on," or to remind us of what they were missing. They became selective in what programs they chose, realizing their choices were limited.

We saw older siblings reading and playing with their young counterparts. They all took a more obvious interest in the daily lives of other family members. No longer did they race through meals and kitchen chores to "see my show."

My real reward came the day seven-year-old Angela came home early from a friend's house complaining, "All she wants to do is watch TV."

All in all, the positive results we have witnessed in our young have made the occasional hassles and nagging well worth the struggle.

Best of all, limiting television viewing leaves more time for REAL leisure. Having guests for dinner, going on picnics (even if just in the backyard) or bringing out the home movies or photo albums — these are the kind of activities that bring parents and children together. And they instill lasting memories that will stay in youngsters' minds far longer than even the most popular sitcom.

# BaseBall
## Dad and Me

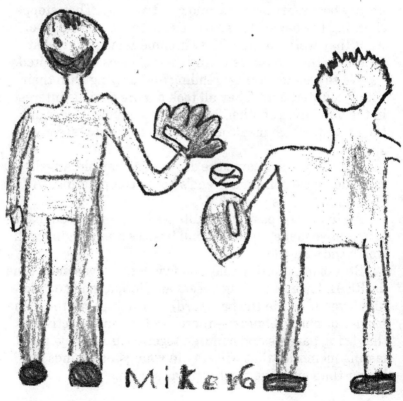

Mike,6

# Chapter 19

# The Game

My husband, a mild-mannered Clark Kent of sorts, neither smokes, drinks (much), chews, or chases. He is affectionate, loving, and considerate in every way. Unless there's a "game." Then he becomes comatose, or takes on the appearance of one completely paralyzed from the eyeballs down, as he sits transfixed, tranquil, and totally mesmerized by "THE GAME."

Enablers like myself quickly recognize the unique language of the sport-aholic. Their greetings to one another may begin with, "Say did you hear what the final score was?" No need to explain what sport, what team, what day, what time, or event. The sport-aholic listener will immediately respond, "Yeh, five to eight in the seventh."

They speak in terms of "seasons." No summer, fall, winter, or spring for them. Rather, their seasons consist of baseball, basketball, football, hockey, tennis, or soccer. The addict gleefully goes from the World Series, to the "Playoffs" to the "Bowls." The only conflict they find is an overlapping of seasons. My guy can sit for hours watching one bowl after another, be it the Superbowl, Sugarbowl, Orangebowl, Cottonbowl, Rosebowl, or the you-name-it-bowl.

Complete withdrawal from being able to watch, listen, or "check to see the score" brings on signs of moodiness, irritability, mumbling, and slurred speech, reddish eyes (tearing at the corners, at least), and an obviously jumpy, jittery, and fidgety behavior. All because he's missing "The Game."

In hindsight, I should have seen it coming when we were dating. I remember one moonlit evening as we sat under the stars, when all thought of cuddling was put on hold as he convincingly pleaded to turn on the radio "just to catch the score." Forty-five minutes later, "the game" was going into overtime and John was shouting at the stars. At the time, blinded by my new-found love, I thought it was cute, and a rather healthy outlet.

I soon came to comprehend that "The Game" conveyed not just baseball or hockey, football or basketball, tennis or volleyball. No. I soon discovered his interest in sports encompassed any or all of the above. Whether the games were played by prominent and paid professionals, or were amateur, yet admirable, academic events, or kids' intermural or Little League sports, if there was a "Game," he was enthralled, enthused, and engrossed.

I had been warned and was rightfully wary of other addictions and afflictions, be they work-aholics or alcoholics. But, is any woman ever properly prepared for marriage to the "sport-aholic"?

There are support groups, clinics, and insurance write offs awaiting those burdened by booze, nicotine, caffeine, abuse, or chemical dependency, or those who are over-weight or under-weight, not to mention a host of empathizing bystanders to offer encouragement. Yet, no such organized society of sympathizers stands ready to soothe a sport-aholic mate's sense of isolation.

If ever there was a reason to cry FOUL this is it.

The male passion to participate, play, or peruse in the pastime of sports seems to pass from fathers to sons, bypassing, except in rare circumstances, the daughters. In spite of this so-called age of "liberation," women are not expected to exhibit the same marked devotion or fanaticism for "the game." Men routinely anticipate such allegiance to "the game" only from their own gender.

And, pity the poor fellow who fails to measure up. He's held suspect — at the least. One naive soul innocently confessed to a sports-minded inquirer, "I don't like the game. I never listen." At which the shocked interrogator responded, "What are ya, a Communist?" After all, every red-blooded, American boy (man) listens to "the game."

I've often felt like a visitor in my own kitchen when

table-talk evolves around the scores, injuries, salaries, or penalties of individuals known only by their last name. "Dad, do you think Herr will be a good trade for Minnesota?" "Did you hear about Bavaro's play?" "What a bummer! Brynanski's leg is going to take six weeks to heal." "I don't think we can pull it off without Kramer in the opening season."

When I occasionally attempt to join in and ask, "What happened to Britannica's leg?" I am either totally ignored or they all look up, note with one swift glance who's doing the asking, and respond in unison, "Never mind. You don't know 'em."

Why can't they talk about the truly meaningful things in life, like fashion, trends, or the latest blue-light special.

Quite frankly, I admire the women who understand "game" talk and ENJOY one or perhaps several sports. Some, like my friend Mary, an admitted football freak, can parlay in pigskin with the likes of any guy. Glued to the tube every Monday night without fail, she knows the names and numbers of all the players. What's most mystifying to me is that not one of them is a relative, close friend, or an acquaintance. I told her my solution to football was to give both sides a ball so they would quit fighting over it. She says I'm hopeless.

I believe my husband has been absorbed in what seems like one continuous game since I've known him. When I come into a room and the TV or radio is on and I inquire, "What are you listening to?" His response is always the same: "THE GAME" — assuming that I would know that it isn't the same "Game" he listened to yesterday, last week, last month, or last season. Whether it's the Vikings, Cowboys, Yanks, North Stars, Dodgers, Super Bowl Sunday, the World Series, or basketball play-offs, it's all summarized as "The Game."

Any reasoned discussion, thoughtful suggestion, innocent inquiry, or life-threatening disaster, is put on hold until either "halftime" or the end of "The Game."

I confess I see no real cure for the sport-aholic and

his/her enabler. I'm hooked on him as much as he's hooked on "The Game."

All in all, give me a sport-aholic man with a mild-mannered nature whose eyes occasionally glaze and glare, and whose being becomes totally captivated and charmed by the lure of leagues. Thankfully, my competition, unlike other addictions, is not food, female, or fatal. And unlike other hopeless addicts, a home run for family always comes first with my sports-minded mate.

# Chapter 20

# The Adorable Incorrigibles

I hate to admit it, but there is a certain amount of truth to the old adage: "Little children — little troubles; bigger children — bigger problems."

"What happens when the adorables become incorrigible?" my friend Renee once kiddingly asked. I can't answer for others, but what works best for my husband and I basically are four ingredients: common sense, trusting our parental instincts, working together, and prayer.

In addition, that marvelous hair-greying method known as "experience" has taught us to establish our ground rules early and to abide by the following guide:

* Be consistent. Nothing confuses a youngster faster than parents who say one thing and then change the rules. Say what you mean and mean what you say. Kids are far more grateful for clear, concise, and consistent standards than for nagging, empty threats, or whimpish warnings, like "Okay, one more chance this time."

* **United we stand or — Fasten your seat belts.** At my wits end over one of my kids, I went to talk with a close friend Vickey, a mother of seventeen children. (I'm not the only nut in the world.) She quietly listened to my problem, asked if Johnny and I were in agreement on how to handle the situation, and then said, "Well kid, man the battle stations, fasten your seat belts, and full speed ahead."

The key word is TOGETHERNESS. Parenting — especially involving a testing or rebellious child, will fall apart and become ten times more difficult, if the parents are at odds. A youngster learns very early if he or she can pit one parent against the other and drive a wedge between father and mother. Each time a child is successful at doing that all parties lose. The child becomes manipulative and disrespectful of authority. In addition, the parents begin to build resentment and animosity toward each other — no longer focusing on the child and his or her shortcomings, but on their mate instead.

Ginny and Gerry's fourteen-year-old Tom was serving detention time in school for his bad behavior and mouthiness. Instead of holding Tom accountable for his actions and insisting he apologize to the teachers he offended, Ginny and Gerry were busy arguing. Tom had successfully managed to manipulate the situation by insinuating that if Gerry showed more appreciation of his son and wasn't so strict Tom would not be so rebellious at school. This tactic was learned many years previously and Ginny fell for it again. The diversionary tactic worked until the trio wound up in family counseling and the game was pointed out to the unsuspecting parents.

**\* Discipline is love.** Love your children enough to discipline them. It's much harder to take the time and energy needed to train a child properly, than to "Let it go." A spanking, grounding, "time-out," taking the car keys, or "whatever works," may be the most loving thing we can do for a disobedient child. It serves as a crucial reminder that our rules and regulations are not meant to hurt but rather to protect them from harm (be it physical, emotional, or spiritual).

One of our sons, a ninth grader at the time, was going through a typical teen, "I'm-old-enough.-Why-can't-I-do-what-I-want" period. On one occasion, as I was explaining the reason behind our latest "No," I looked up in time to catch sight of his teeth-clenching, eyes blazing, defiance. I stopped what I was unsuccessfully trying to say and simply said in the softest, most loving voice I could muster, "I know it's hard for you to understand why, but you know that we are motivated by LOVE and nothing more. We would never intentionally hurt you, nor do we want you to be miserable, unhappy, or denied — just for the sake of being mean. We love you and we're only doing what we think is for your best welfare."

At that point, he looked up. His eyes softened and his body became limp, as he quietly nodded, "I know you love me, mom." End of confrontation. He remained unconvinced of my position and still wanted his way, but the arguing and hostility were gone.

To a rebellious child, reminders of love are extremely important.

* **TLC — Tenderness, love and closeness.** All children have a need for closeness and touching. When kids enter their teen years, there may be a tendency to forget or forgo this. With boys especially, it is sometimes sadly assumed, "He's getting too old for that now." On the contrary, we all need affection. Teenagers, faced with over-active hormones, challenges, decisions, and temptations to rebel, even more need to feel their parents' tenderness and love.

I discovered many kids ago that while I may never appreciate their hair styles, music, or teen tastes, the lines of communication would always be open as long as I kept extending that warm hug, motherly kiss and tender pat. On occasion, I've even hugged kids right after a stormy discussion, grounding, or disciplinary action. It lessens the tension, adds an ounce of mercy, and demonstrates forgiveness.

* **The importance of touching and hugging.** One of my friends told of a particularly obstinate teen whose language and behavior was becoming increasingly obnoxious and abusive. In seeking outside help, all but one counselor told the mother her only hope was to evict the boy when he turned eighteen.

One consultant, however, insisted she cease all verbal communication, yet not let a day pass without giving her son a hug. The first week passed, and the only change in the boy was that his language had become less offensive. He showed no outward sign, however, of encouraging, or even tolerating the physical contact. He pushed her away.

"After two weeks of virtually forcing a daily hug I saw no real warmth or change," recalled my friend. "Late one evening at the end of the second week, however, he came up behind me when I was reading the newspaper. He stood in the doorway with his pajamas on. When I looked up and saw his hulkish, six-foot frame in the door, I asked him what he was looking for. He shrugged and sheepishly said, 'Aren't you forgetting something?' (referring to the 'Good Night' hug I'd usually given him)."

It worked! "Where talking, screaming, crying, and nagging had done nothing but aggravate the hostile situation, a daily hug had melted hearts and broken down the barriers."

**\* Don't delay or postpone punishment.** If a child, no matter the age, has done something to merit parental discipline, the punishment should be swift, merciful, and, after the youngster's apology and promise to be good, forgotten. Neither mother nor father should bully a youngster by postponing the punishment with a, "Just wait until your father gets home," or waiting for a future date too difficult for the child to connect to the offense.

Preschoolers *usually* comprehend a swift swat on the bottom far better than being denied something an hour or two later — never use an object, however, a hand is stern enough.

Spanking is usually ineffective on a school-age child and could be a source of humiliation unequal to the wrongdoing. We have found that enforcing "time out" penalties, or grounding (not being permitted to leave his room, or the family property), works on most youngsters, except the very young) and is far more beneficial. This technique may give a child just the "break" needed to re-think his or her behavior and the time needed to decide to make the desired change. It gives mom and dad a cooling-off period, too.

To show his unhappiness over Joseph, his new baby brother, Dominic, then a wiry three, was into endless mischief. We tried spanking him, and denying him treats, yet nothing seemed to work. Finally, we had him sit in a chair, on the stairs, or in his room, depending on the offense. At minimum, he was isolated from playing with the others. That did the trick.

After a respectable period of time, he would call out, "Mama, can I be a nice boy now?" I sometimes whispered under my breath, "Is that possible?" The change for this spunky tot didn't come easy. It took numerous trips to the stairs and his room before the "time out" and isolation got through where the wallops had failed.

* **Praise and punishment go hand in hand.** When a youngster, especially one who knows better and yet "chooses" to do wrong, is in trouble, that should be seen by parents for what it is — a cry for help. They want to be noticed, loved, and respected. My husband and I believe this is as true of three-year-olds demonstrating jealousy over a new baby, as it is of teenagers trying to "make a statement."

Discipline, when done lovingly, answers that need. On the other hand, you don't want to set up a situation where a child remembers that the negative attention seems to get the strongest reaction from his parents. If that's the case, he or she will head for more of the same.

* **Keep 'em busy.** When our kids are being punished for bad behavior, we not only ground them, but we give them something to do. My husband tells them, "You must have lots of energy to burn and not enough to do, because if you did have enough to do, you wouldn't have time to get in trouble. So grab a bucket and vacuum and we'll make a list of some of the things around here you can help with."

Depending upon the offense, the age of the child, and the situation, the setting up of additional chores does three things: 1. It keeps a child busy. The old adage: "Idle hands are the devil's tools," is certainly true. 2. The work helps him or her burn off some of that energy and frustration. 3. It gives the parent something for which to thank and praise the kid. Thus, the child is reminded that not everything he does is bad and his folks do recognize and appreciate the good in him even if done as a punishment.

* **Your home is your castle.** We believe a home and what is spoken, listened to, read and seen in it, is a reflection of the people who live there. For that reason, we tell

our youngsters — including those college-age, young adults — that we cannot permit material that is indecent, offensive, or that contradicts our faith and values. This includes albums, tapes, television shows, videos, magazines, books, and even comics. To tolerate such material is really an inadvertent way of condoning it.

As long as children, adult or otherwise, live at home, they must be respectful and reverent of parental authority and rules — including religious practices. Our kids go to church with us unless part-time work or a special occasion prevent it. And even then, they are required to go to church on their own.

**\* Everyone needs to feel valuable — Give 'em a job.** Even small children want to feel an active part of the family. If everything is done FOR them, they feel more like a guest than family.

My friend Kathy was experiencing adjustment problems with one of the three children she and her husband recently adopted from South America. One boy (age nine) was in constant trouble and being punished — with no good results. Having been there a few times myself, I could more than sympathize.

"Do you have a dishwasher?" I asked her.

"Well, yes," she said. "But what's that got to do with Peter's acting up?" "Put that energetic little guy to work every day. Don't use the dishwasher. Make him in charge of doing the dishes and insist all the kids make their beds, keep their rooms clean, and help with the chores. Be sure to compliment them when they do good — most especially Peter."

After protesting that "he might break every dish in the house," Kathy decided she had nothing to lose and gave it a try. Two weeks later she called to tell me of Peter's improvement. "He still has his moments, but the rebellious, antagonistic behavior was gone," she said. "He takes great pride in his work and you can just see that it makes him feel needed and vital to our family."

Adoption adjustment or otherwise, even in small

families, no child should grow up without specific chores to do EVERY DAY. Even small tasks help begin the formation of a good work ethic. While giving a child an allowance may have its place (we never got into that — our kids had paper routes and babysitting jobs to obtain spending money), no child should be paid for every little effort made. Everyone should contribute toward making their home and surroundings clean and comfortable.

\* **Pick your battles.** All teens need to do something a little off the wall or outrageous. Better they do it now while they are young and protected by mom and dad, then do it in their 20s, 30s, or 40s and ruin a relationship with a spouse, children, or their home life because of a foolish or careless act.

While some parental rules and requests cannot waiver, others can be bent with little harm. For instance, we had a rule that our kids clothes and hair had to be respectful and decent (in our judgment — not theirs).

One year, when our son Tim was a testy tenth-grader, he had been pushing for a weird haircut. He was an A student, obedient, and faithfully worked his part-time job and at-home chores. I wanted no such haircut before grandma and grandpa's big fiftieth wedding anniversary celebration at which we would be host to over one hundred of our relatives and friends. Let's face it. I wanted to show the kid off. The very next day after our "discussion," Tim went out and had his hair cut — with the sides shaved off completely, with a "lightening bolt" patch emblazoned over the ears. "Awful" is the only word to describe it. A gang leader on the prowl had more class.

On the other hand, compared to taking drugs, illicit sex, skipping school, drinking, smoking, or sassing teachers, the "Lightening Bolt Kid" looked like an angel, once I sat down and thought about it. Luckily I saw him at a distance and had a few minutes to collect my shock. When he came in the door, I asked, "Does this make you happy?" Tim answered, "Yup."

Like it or not, he looked like most of his sophomore class

that year. I put my arms around him, told him I thought it was terrible and gave him a big hug and kiss. Once it grew out, he never cut his hair like that again. I lost the battle, but won the war!

* **Prayer, prayer, and more prayer.** Being a parent has a way of intensifying prayer life. At least it has in our lives.

I don't have all the answers, and as a temperamental Italian, I've been known to flash a short fuse on tense occasions. My constant prayer is that I be a good parent to my children.

Even at that, there are trying times when my worries or frustration over a kid may have me on edge with that "What'll-he-do-next" feeling. Whether it's a "terrible two"-year-old, or a rebellious teen, there are times even the best of parents feel little love or affection for a defiant youngster.

The simple prayer that helps me through is, "Lord, help me see them through your eyes and not mine." It's amazing how that thought breaks down the built-up bias, and brings back the tenderness.

The way I see it, these are God's children and He must love them a great deal more than we do — and that's a lot. So when the going gets rough, as it does at one time or another, we turn to our Heavenly Creator for guidance — if not for STRENGTH!

* **When all else fails, don't be afraid to ask for help.** Sometimes, no matter how good the parents, how consistent the rules, how heroic the efforts made, or how diligent the prayers, a continuously troubled youth may need the influence and input of a third party. At times it goes past the point of advice from good friends. Then it's time to call a trusted priest, religious, or the child's school counselor. If those avenues fail, then it's time to seek professional counseling. The important thing to remember is to choose one that is respectful of your religious and moral view.

* **Admit your error and apologize when you are wrong.** Hopefully only God is keeping track of the number

of times I have flown off the handle, over-reacted, or judged a situation too harshly. I have, on occasion, had to apologize to a child, admitting my error or haste. What a wonderful outcome has resulted. Perhaps it is times such as these that our children learn even more from parents about humility, compassion, forgiveness and remorse.

What do we do when the adorable become incorrigible? The answer, at our house is, "Fasten your seat belt and just love 'em."

*Chapter 21*

# Chastity — Straight Talk To Teens

Teens seem to have a sixth sense for ferreting out those who tell them to do one thing, but EXPECT they will do another. Most can smell a phony or hypocritical message a mile away.

In fact, nothing is more disappointing and confusing to young people than being sold short and made to feel they can't live up to a standard.

Never was this more evident than when drug education "experts" taught the concept of "responsible use" rather than telling youngsters to reject drugs altogether. Sadly, it has taken the ravages of a decade of escalated chemical and alcohol abuse amongst teens to teach adults the most elementary lesson, namely, that you can't tell young people, "Don't. But if you do, at least do it 'responsibly.' " They hear only the underlying message, "At least do it responsibly" — or worse, "We know you can't resist."

Tragically, that old misguided approach is now being used to teach children about pregnancy, VD, and AIDS prevention. Adolescents are being hyped with yet another double message — "Don't. But if you do, protect yourself."

Perhaps the biggest disappointment about this method of education, is the public's willingness to let it happen. Society would never tolerate a driver education instructor who taught "alternatives" to safe and lawful driving, i.e., "speed or drink but use a fuzz-buster so you don't get caught." Nor would we hire an educator whose classroom instruction was not clearly opposed to shoplifting, robbery, rape, and homicidal acts.

Today, more than ever, parents, educators, the religious community, and even the government, must recognize the over-riding and compelling interest in teaching the

Judeo/Christian principle of chastity. Society itself has an obligation to protect young people from exploitation and abuse. The very real threat of statutory rape, venereal disease, pregnancy, and AIDS can leave long-lasting, if not life-threatening, scars. In essence, there is no place for a "values-free" or neutral position. Teens need and want guidelines.

Chastity is the only effective educational and principled approach which will instill a healthy self-image, create a strong concept of self and others, and protect our young from personal disaster.

Even for Christian parents, talking to our children about sexual intimacy can be awkward or difficult in finding the "right words." With some of my young, I've handed them someone else's words first — through a pamphlet, book, or an article on Church teaching — using it as my "foot in the door" to open the discussion. The older I get the more I believe, however, that it doesn't matter so much what we say, but rather how we live — the chaste example we set for them — as well as letting them feel our love and the confidence we have in their ability to choose good.

As far as specifics, we begin by letting our teens know:

* **You are a special person.** In all the world there is no one quite like you. Each human being is made in the image and likeness of God. That is why we must strive to treat all others, even those we may not personally like, as someone special — the way we would want to be treated.

* **Your sexuality is part of the "gift" of your being.** Sexual intercourse, "making love," is something so profound, so powerful, and so beautiful that it must be protected by the marriage covenant. To use it outside of marriage, whether for personal satisfaction, or in payment for favors received from another, or even as a symbol of love, is to cheapen and abuse this God-given gift. In other words, if it is given away, treated as little more than a handshake or sensual urge to be satisfied, it is no longer the "special gift" God intended.

Sex outside of marriage is a clear violation of God's plan for the family and may seriously endanger your physical, spiritual, and personal well-being. The Bible tells us in Exodus 20:14: "You Shall not commit adultery." And in the New Testament (1 Cor 6:9-10), we are warned:

"Do you not know that the unjust will not inherit the kingdom of God? Do not be deceived; neither fornicators nor idolaters nor adulterers nor boy prostitutes nor practicing homosexuals nor thieves nor the greedy nor drunkards nor slanderers nor robbers will inherit the kingdom of God."

In fact, there is no organized, respected religion in the United States which condones sex outside of marriage. Both Christians and Jews teach that this act is a physical expression of the love between husband and wife, and because each act of intercourse is open to the possibility of new life, it is to be guarded and protected within the confines of the stable, ongoing, and committed relationship that can only come in marriage.

* **There is no such thing as "safe sex" outside of marriage.** It is dangerous and deceptive to promote contraceptives to assure freedom from risk. Every sexual act is open to the possibility of pregnancy, venereal disease, sexually transmitted diseases and AIDS, as any counselor in a pregnancy clinic can testify. Remember, ONLY abstinence works one hundred percent. Don't let anyone talk you out of the gift of your sexuality.

* **Chastity is the true test of love.** A date who really cares about YOU would deny himself or herself sexual satisfaction, in order to be sure you would be free from any dangers, risk, or harm. Chastity builds mutual confidence and respect and assures you that your mate values the whole you and not just the sexual urges you have in common.

Everyone — whether single or married — is called by God to live chaste and pure lives and to reject sinful, impure, or unlawful sexual activity.

* **Chastity gives you freedom.** Making a decision to abstain from sexual intimacy until marriage will virtually

guarantee you a life free of AIDS, herpes, and VD, and the risk of pregnancy. There will be no guilt and shame as from promiscuous sex, all of which add up to the genuine freedom which a peaceful conscience alone can provide.

* **It's never too late for chastity.** Even if you've failed in the past, it is never too late to change, and to choose standards and principles that will help make you a happier and more "in-control" person. God will forgive you and will give you the grace you need to live a chaste and happy life. You need only ask.

Thousands of others, after experiencing the let-down of being sexually promiscuous, have turned to a life of chastity and abstinence and discovered the great joy and freedom of REALLY "controlling their own body" and not being a slave to temporary emotions. Animals can't say, "No." Human beings have free will and self-control.

* **We believe in you.** The Church, your family, your teachers, and so many others, know that being chaste is not always easy, but you can do it. Being chaste is being obedient to God's laws, your parents, and your own high standards.

* **Being chaste demonstrates loyalty.** Chastity demonstrates self-control and a degree of trustworthiness and faithfulness that will carry over even AFTER marriage. Your marriage partner will know you can be trusted, because you were trustworthy before marriage.

You are, by your actions, telling your dates that you reserve the gift of your sexuality for that one special person — your marriage partner. Your chastity will truly be a "gift of love."

* **Set your standards high and know that others will respect you and think more of you for it.** It takes a real man or woman of courage, discipline, and determination to say, "Not me, I'm saving myself for marriage." Setting high standards, and looking for a partner who has the same values, will gain you the respect of others.

* **Promise yourself that your dress, language, and actions will show respect for your body and for**

**others.** Remember, dressing immodest (tight, scanty, or revealing) clothes, the use of "filthy" language, or hanging out with kids who are into drugs or drinking gives others the wrong message.

The use of alcohol and drugs is not only illegal and dangerous, but it weakens your self-control. Being with the "in" crowd is NEVER worth a ruined reputation or the stigma of an arrest.

* **Plan your dates well.** Let your standards be known. A date should know without asking that you are a person who values your body, your sexuality, and the gift of chastity.

A good rule of thumb: Double date whenever possible. Keep things light. Temptation is strongest when lights are low, emotions are strong, and no one else is around.

* **A kiss and affection are something special.** Don't give away affection unless you are sincere. Remember petting, sexual experimentation, and sexual intercourse outside of marriage are wrong. It is also selfish and tells the other, "I want it NOW and I won't wait. Who cares about YOU or the outcome." Real love always puts self last and the welfare of the other first.

* **Think ahead.** Before acting on impulse think of God, your parents, your family, and your future. Ask yourself, "Would my mom and dad approve of my behavior?" "How does God ask me to live?" "What kind of a lifetime partner do I want, and is chastity a mutual gift I want to bring and receive in marriage?" "How will I feel about myself later?"

* **Pray, stay close to your faith.** God's grace will help you withstand all temptations and occasions that may be sinful. His grace is always more powerful than any situation. God calls us to a life of chastity — even after marriage, and He gives us the means to achieve this goal. We need only ask His help.

The teens of today might just prove to be some of the finest of any generation. Many have withstood the permissive, yet worn-thin abuses of the "sexual revolution," and the empty promises of TV, video, film, teen idols, and, "values-free" educators, in order to hold onto the cherished goal of saving themselves for marriage. This in itself demonstrates an openness to truth and principle. In fact, even a recent (1987) Planned Parenthood poll of people age twelve to seventeen revealed that "only twenty-eight percent had sexual intercourse. In other words, seventy-two percent of high schoolers are attempting to live chaste lives.

Indeed, many of today's young prove by their actions that they can rise to great acts of self-sacrifice and self-denial, especially for the good of another.

We do teens a great injustice and disservice, then, when we short-change them in the area of sexuality, encouraging failure by offering a double-messaged con program. This approach ignores their ability to be in control of their sexuality and to deny themselves for their own sake and for the welfare of others.

Today's young deserve no less than our enthusiastic support, prayers, and responsible guidance.

TEENS
Mary age-13

cooler

# Chapter 22

# The Growing Pains Of Teenage Boys

My son Tim is smiling again. A sweetness has re-surfaced and he's actually fun to have around. There were times I thought we'd never see his grin or that cute twinkle in his eye again. At times I was sure he had regressed to little more than a pan-face stoic, responding to most anyone daring to approach, with rarely more than a nod, grunt, or inaudible groan.

Tim, our first-born son, was the boy who at age three and four, would crawl up on my lap and cuddle, stopping me from my reading or work by saying, "I think I need a little hug." Who could resist?

At five or six he could be heard throughout the house humming nursery and kindergarten rhymes — a happy-go-lucky, always cheerful, little chap who loved to fill his pockets with matchbox cars, key chains, and gadgets.

Through grade school, his naturally shy nature was never over-shadowed by his fun-loving ways and dry (like his father's) sense of humor.

By the time Tim hit thirteen, he was an industrious paper carrier and loved spending Saturdays on his grandpa's farm, spreading hay and even shoveling manure. He was the kind of kid who just looked pleased with life in general.

And then puberty and the teenage years came. I'm not sure when the change occurred, if it was gradual or just overnight. All I know is that he went from a boy full of energy and an eagerness to an awkward fifteen-year-old who became moody and withdrawn, serious and sullen. That once boundless energy and enthusiasm was now rationed between school activities and peers with little left for home and family.

When he was young, no task was too great. After puberty, no task was small enough. Asking Tim to take out the trash received about the same resistance as if I had told him to clean ten dirty diapers, move a mountain, or worse yet — clean his room.

At that age his usual response to most chores was, "It's not my turn," "That's Charlie's job," or "Why does it always have to be me?"

Laziness and no pep is all I can remember about his sophomore year of high school. His interests were reserved for sports, TV, constant noise (rock music), more TV and "sleeping in." Being the difficult parents that we are, we set limits on the television, and instituted a 9:00 A.M. "Wake up call" for weekends and summertime — a rule that didn't set well with anyone who was up late the night before.

"Sleeping in after nine is unhealthy," I would tell our teens. "You can sleep all day when you're in your own apartment." A tempting thought to all of us.

By age sixteen, Tim had reached the age of the strange hair-do's, clothes that "made a statement," and ideas thrown out that helped turn John's hair thin and mine in need of a "rinse." We realized early on that if he WASN'T doing something a bit outrageous, we'd better worry. With that in mind we gratefully accepted the haircut with the lightening bolt emblazoned in shaved skin over the ear, the "macho" posters on his wall, and the nasal twanging sounds drifting from his bedroom of Bob Dylan (a 60s hippie who was popular when we were in our prime and "making our statement").

Under the chopped hair, mammoth sneakers, and oversized coat *a la* "Ragstock," still sat our Tim.

The hairdo and the clothes I could accept. It was the sullen face with the perpetual scowl and the moody undercurrent that made us think Mount St. Helen's was more predictable and probably more serene.

"I can't believe this kid is my sweet-natured, once-lovable Tim," I confessed to my friend Pat one day.

"Don't worry. He'll get over it. Give him some time and

space. They're unsure of so many things at that age," she advised.

"Remember, teenagers have to work very hard to look 'cool' all the time," Pat counseled. "It's not an age to show happiness, or to be sociable and approving of parents. Good grief. He'd be an outcast with his friends."

Pat, who had already lived through five teenagers and survived, helped me understand it was Tim's time to question. "They question parental authority, question rules they once automatically followed, and even challenge thoughts and values previously accepted as gospel."

"They don't smile often during this period because there is so much on their mind," she explained, "like school, friendships, dating, college plans, career choices, and that scary unknown future."

With all that on their minds, it's a wonder they smile at all. Looking back, perhaps the best thing I did for Tim during this "questioning" period in his life, was to pray the Rosary for him.

It's a time of growing, but not without pain. In addition to the lanky legs, changed voices, and run-away hormones, it is a time of self-searching rather than soul-searching, as they discover who they are and who they will strive to become.

In addition, we noticed an eagerness for withdrawal and privacy. In our family, the closed bedroom door seems to mark the onset of a kid beginning his or her teen transition. With Tim, conversation and communication was put on hold. When we'd ask the simple: "What did you do today?" we got the usual, "Nothing."

Indeed, an "I dunno," a shrug, or a grunt was the "normal" (??) response to virtually everything we asked.

For Tim, and most teens, there was also the need to feel in complete conformity with their peers.

Here's where we lucked out. Tim's peers came from some of the nicest families we knew. In fact, we loved his choice of friends as if they were (as we often joked) our "adopted sons."

Of course, there were some fun moments, during those years, but it normally occurred when we were involved in things that Tim liked to do: swimming, vacationing, going to grandma's cabin, and waterskiing, learning to drive, and getting the use of the family car.

We had entered the era of "navel gazing," when most of his thoughts, plans, dreams, and fears revolved around him. At this age there is as much concern over an erupting zit, as the quandary over whether or not to show for the school dance.

With Tim we were very blessed. We never had bouts with alcohol, drugs, gangs, or sex. He was a good boy. And yet, his attitude toward others became indifferent. He had mood swings marked with irritability, and seemed to only be tolerating the existence of the human race.

On several heated occasions, when our tempers got testy, I told him he was free to leave when he reached eighteen. He always looked like he could hardly wait. The feeling was only too mutual.

And then senior year came, and with it a boy who began to change. Gone were the sour looks, the sullen face, and the stoic attitude. While he didn't offer to pitch in and help, he no longer argued about the household tasks asked of him. He began to speak in whole sentences, his attention span lasted longer than thirty seconds, and eyes that once seemed glued to the floor were soft and attractive. In fact, once in a while we saw a smile and a chuckle.

The first time I knew the cold-war was over was the same evening I realized we had lost a teenager but gained a "young adult." We were at Tim's baccalaureate dinner and he leaned over and said, "You've really changed over this past year, mom. You've really eased up on us and seem to trust us so much more." I was delighted that he noticed. Yet, I had not done the changing. He had. In spite of his non-communicative behavior, he had been obedient (most of the time) to our curfews and family rules. He had proven his trustworthiness, and as a result, had earned our trust and a softening of restraints that offered a new-found freedom.

A year later, it was I who noticed a big change. At nineteen, and a college sophomore, Tim was occasionally OFFERING to pitch in and help around the house. He seemed kinder, nicer, more gentle, and more comfortable with us. He took time with his young brothers and sisters, who devotedly look up to him. Gone was the scowl, the chip on the shoulder, and the "Why me?" response. He no longer groaned under his breath when we'd announce it was time for the evening Rosary! Best of all, he seemed genuinely happy to be a member of the family.

"There is life after fourteen, after all" I told myself. And now it's Tim's kid brother, Tony, who mumbles in inaudible grunts, walks with a "cool" swagger, and hasn't cracked a smile since he began shutting his bedroom door.

"He looks like he hates everybody," one of our other kids said in describing Tony one day.

"He doesn't really hate anybody. He's just put his sense of humor on hold for a while."

Thank heavens Tim prepared me. At least I know it's only temporary.

# Chapter 23

# Chrissy: The Dependable Child

I get a certain twinge in the corner of my heart every time I hear the Bible story about the "Prodigal son." I'm not so much thinking of the son-come-home. I'm sure we can all relate, either because of our own past deeds or that of another's, to the unconditional love and forgiveness it takes to welcome home a repentant family member. Yet, it's the other child that gets me.

The parable makes me reflect on my own family and while it gives me genuine hope for those who may become wayward, I'm thinking of the uncelebrated, loyal, dependable, obedient child who never causes anxiety or heartache.

As Jesus tells the story (Luke 15:11-32): There was a man who had two sons. The younger asked for his share of the estate and went off to a distant land, "where he squandered his inheritance" on dissolute living. After he spent everything, he came to his senses and returned home to beg his father's forgiveness.

The father, overjoyed at his prodigal son's return, clothed the boy in the finest robe, shoes, and ring, and told his servants to kill the fatted calf for a big celebration.

When the elder son returned from a day in the field and saw the music and dancing, he became angry and told his father, "Look, all these years I served you and not once did I disobey your orders; yet you never gave me even a young goat to feast on with my friends. But when your son returns who swallowed up your property with prostitutes, for him you slaughter the fatted calf."

His father's response was "My son, you are here with me always; everything I have is yours. But now we must celebrate and rejoice, because your brother was dead and has come to life again; he was lost and has been found."

Speaking as an experienced and biased mom, all my children are extraordinarily good. But there's one in particular who never seems to groan, complain, or resist a parental request. In my family, her name is Chrissy and I shudder at the thought that in my haste to mother, nurture, and mop up after others, she may not fully realize how much we "celebrate" her very existence and the beautiful virtues that make her such a delight to our lives.

She is the oldest of our many children and seems to just naturally take upon her shoulders the special burdens and duties at which others might rightfully protest or rebel.

From a very young age, she tended to have a "Mother Hen" approach toward the siblings in our brood. When she was little, she showed it in small ways. Most youngsters seem to naturally horde and hide little treats they receive. Not Chrissy. Her enjoyment came when she could "share it with others." There was the time she rode the bus home from kindergarten and eagerly unwrapped a napkin holding two oversized cookies she had saved from a classroom Valentine party in order to share (split six ways!!!) with her younger brothers and sisters.

On one not-to-be-forgotten occasion, we discovered how much she treasured her designated spot in the family. It was the spring of 1975. Just days after we were notified that our newly adopted son, Daniel Thanh, (six and one-half), was killed in a plane crash as he was being airlifted to us from Vietnam, our caseworker called to tell us about several other adoptable little girls. All, however, were older than Chrissy.

When Chrissy heard of the possibility of a big sister, she burst into tears and said, "But I like being the oldest. Aren't there other families they can go to?" Realizing that being "the oldest" meant that much to Chrissy, we called the adoption worker back and were relieved to learn that the children in question had all been placed. "But, would you consider a little boy (age five and one-half)?" she then asked. We certainly would, and in a few days we had a new son. We also learned in the process never again to threaten the "reign supreme" of our "oldest-by-choice" child.

Through her growing up years, which brought with it dramatic changes in the size and shape of our family, she never failed to be a good role model, mentor, and friend to the younger children in our crew.

And on occasion, when mutiny threatened or others were "in the dog house," or absent-without-cause, Chrissy was dependable. During the times that some, by their wayward ways, captured our attention and demanded our time, Chrissy faithfully pulled her load, ignoring the distractions and resisting the temptation to create her own spotlight.

Chrissy, like many an older and reliable child, seems to possess an unfailing sixth sense for responding to the needs of others. It's just not her nature to "Look out for Number One" as the contemporary "Me-first" slogan goes.

Of course, there were occasions when she balked at household tasks and chores. And there were times when she objected to parental rules and early curfews. Yet, when "negotiations" failed her, she was obedient.

When a bike trip with college friends fell on the same weekend as her kid sister's graduation, she certainly wrestled over the dilemma. Yet in the end, she stayed home to clean and help with the family party. Never mind that she had looked forward to the weekend for months.

This is the child who is loyal and obedient, but much more. She's the big sister most of her sibling brothers and sisters may never fully realize was the one who so often stopped to tie their shoes, bathe their sandbox-dirtied bodies, read stories to them for hours on end, and shower them with treats she brought home "just for them." Most of the other kids are too small to appreciate what a good thing they have going in this larger-than-life "Big sister."

Looking back on the story of the Prodigal Son, I see little by way of real comparison between Chrissy and the older brother. She's harbored no anger or resentment over the affection or attention we've shown the others in our care. Where I see a similarity is in her quiet obedience and faithfulness. Of course, we can't kill a fatted calf, and we won't slight a prodigal child who demands our attention with his or her serious or immediate needs. But what we can do, is occasionally take the time to celebrate with that older and loyally obedient child.

Many parents have a Chrissy in their life. When's the last time you took her to lunch, surprised her with a small gift or just leaned over and said, "Thank you for the blessing you are to our lives."

going to college

Angela
Age 9

# Chapter 24

# She Took A Bit Of Home
# When She Left

Watching an adopted child leave home brought to mind memories and feelings that hadn't surfaced in years.

It wasn't easy saying goodbye to our eighteen-year-old, college-bound Tina. As we unloaded her prize possessions (enough clothes to outfit her for all four years, plus a graduate and post-graduate stay), we embraced and exchanged last-minute instructions: Me, "If you need anything call us and remember we love you" and Tina, "Yes, mom. Don't worry. And remember to keep the kids out of my stuff." (What "stuff?" I thought she took it all!)

Resurrecting an old Catholic custom, I made a small sign of the cross on her young and wrinkle-free forehead, gave her my blessing, and grabbed and kissed her one last time. She was doing what she had planned and dreamed of for years — "going away to college" and we were loving her enough to let her go. But it wasn't easy. She would leave behind an irreplaceable void.

While we may offer some help to our college-bound young adults, Johnny and I believe it is primarily *their* responsibility and not ours to provide for their college education. Our only promise to our high-school grads is free room and board if they live at home and go to college. Tina's older sister and two brothers chose an in-town college. Tina prepared for the financial challenge of college well in advance. She gathered a nest egg of savings from working as a paper carrier, babysitter, and various part-time jobs during her high school years. In addition, she signed up for the student work program and received a generous scholarship. To Tina, the cost of going to a private college was well worth the price.

It's funny how watching a child leave home — whether to pursue a career, marriage, or going away to school, can trigger in a parent, all sorts of memories that hadn't surfaced in years. Somehow we realize that when they leave — even if it's just a temporary nine-month stint at school — that it's a giant first step to independence, and their returns will be short, fleeting, and never quite the same.

My friend Joan readily conceded her own "mild depression" and adjustment after her two daughters (both adopted as infants) went away to college. "I was surprised that I actually went into such a depression, first with Michele and even more so when Sheila, our second daughter left home and the nest was entirely empty. I was a busy and very fulfilled person and felt very prepared, but I wasn't. It was hard not to have our family together. I still remember the first Easter alone. It was a real adjustment."

Nancy, another friend, who has had three children leave home helped prepare me. She said that "when they're packing their lifetime treasures it is really more for security," kind of like Linus and his blanket. "They seem to do better," she said, "feeling they have a bit of home with them." I felt better, too.

As we drove our stuffed mini-van to St. Ben's College in St. Joseph, Minnesota, the school she had dreamed of attending for years, my mind drifted backward reliving Tina's first entrance into our lives. She was our third child, the first one to come (as the kids used to say), not by "tummy" but by "airport" and adoption.

After waiting for well over a year, which included a series of setbacks and false arrivals, Tina stepped into our lives through the grace of a last minute Visa granted by the Department of Immigration. It was 1972 and Philippine President Ferdinand Marcos had just issued his Marshall Law edict which virtually halted out-of-country travel. By this time our discouraged adoption case worker told us to "give her up — We may never get her out." We refused. Instead we waited and prayed. Soon it was Christmas time, and after receiving a two-day notice of her possible arrival, we half-believingly met her 5:00 A.M. plane, December 16th. And there she was! After a twenty-six-hour flight our eighteen-month-old Christmas present had come. We cried with joy all the way home.

It didn't take long to realize, as perhaps every adoptive and foster parent does, that bonding and love is not automatic. We had to earn our way into Tina's heart.

Having spent her first month of life with her mother, the next fourteen months in an orphanage, and the last three in foster care, she was not open to trusting yet another new home or "mother." For Tina and many adopted children there were other mothers and other caretakers, and each time they disappeared from their young lives, the ability to trust diminished.

Taking her now to this new and strange college home, reminded me of those first years together. I remembered the trauma and her eventual adjustment. How playful and responsive she was in the daytime, yet evenings brought nightmares and uncontrollable crying. Each time it happened we could do little more than hold her, sing to her, and wait until she fell, exhausted, back to sleep. Adoption does take time.

I called her my little "Rosebud" because she was so tight and closed to any overtures of intimacy and affection. There were days when we worried, and wondered out loud if she'd ever know how much we loved her or would let us into her locked up little heart. Only as the months and years passed did she begin to unfold and blossom, revealing a beautiful, little person bursting with affection and love. Yet she rationed this to a select few in her accepted inner circle. As she grew, her circle widened and so did her ability to love and accept the love of others.

Once she entered school, her talent and skill at piano recitals, class plays, volunteer projects, and varsity sports, portrayed an outward charm and self-confidence, which neatly hid a diminishing, yet still self-conscious, insecurity. We thrilled with each progressive step.

In between the steps, and most importantly, a strong

mother-daughter bond was forming. I remembered the day I went to watch Tina perform in a class play. I arranged for a neighbor to watch my preschoolers and breathlessly rushed to her school. When I arrived, I was surprised to discover this was an in-school event and I was the ONLY parent present in the third grade classroom.

As I watched the roomful of eight-year-olds act out the sad and serious story, I noticed a smile virtually pasted across Tina's almond-skinned face. Tina was playing Maria in the martyrdom of St. Maria Goretti and her gleeful expression made little sense in connection with the role she was portraying. I sat puzzled in my third-grade chair wondering, "Why the smile?" Before the play ended, the teacher leaned over the row of children's desks where my legs awkwardly hung out and whispered in my ear, "It must have meant a great deal to Tina to have you come today. I've never seen her smile before. She's a good little girl but always so solemn. She's obviously so thrilled that her mother's here she can't contain her delight." Nor could I. I cried all the way home.

In high school, her excellence in sports earned her several letters, and her continued interest in theater landed her parts in the school plays of *The Sound of Music*, *Oklahoma*, and *Oliver*. All this added to her sense of accomplishment and self-confidence and nurtured a vigorous interest in old show tunes and musicals.

At home, she avoided additional chores and frowned on "unnecessary" cleaning. Yet she doted on "the little girls," her sisters, ages eleven, nine, and eight. It was always Tina they looked to when they wanted their hair curled, fingernails painted, or clothes designed for a party or neighborhood parade.

She was also our resident baker and gourmet. She loved to tease about my old-fashioned ways like never using the dishwasher, and telling them, "I have thirteen dishwashers already." And when grandma bought us a microwave, she always reminded me that I called it "the heater" and had to ask HER how to use it.

We all grew and easily survived her delicate phase of adolescence and tender teen years, including its stages of withdrawal, mood-swings, and the yearning for aloneness and privacy. What eventually emerged with Tina was the blossoming of an affectionate, warm, and loving young lady. A far different personality than the one that came into our lives so many years back. What more could we ask?

The college admissions director, in speaking frankly to the parents said, "Your children are here to get an education. In addition, leaving home is an ENORMOUS step toward eventual independence. At the end of their four years here, parents must expect that their children will leave far different than when they came." I gulped hard on that one.

I'm sure that letting go of an adopted child is no different than a "tummy" kid. It's just that our beginning bonds with Tina were more fragile and our efforts to be a family more purposeful. It didn't just happen. We had to work and want it to happen.

Now it was time to trust and believe that nothing could erase or diminish — no matter the distance or circumstance — the ties and bond of love that unites us. After all, she "took a bit of home" when she left.

# Chapter 25

# Living With Adult Children

"Where do we go from here?" was the question that summed up our feelings as we entered the new world of "parents with adult children living at home." It was an experience uninviting, unknown, and certainly unfamiliar. For the sake of our "kids" (not a term they always appreciate), as well as our own peace of mind, we were determined to find a common ground that would be clear, comfortable, and congenial for all of us.

"It seems like only yesterday," I told a friend, "when I walked my two small sons up the street to enroll them in kindergarten."

Tim, one of our "tummy kids" had shared his life, his bedroom, and school-year experiences with Charlie, our son who came to us by adoption at age five and one-half from Vietnam. Their high school graduation marked a new beginning in their still young lives.

Both boys had chosen to go to colleges within driving distance of home. Thus we knew that once the "after grad" parties and celebrations were over, it was time to sit down and lay some ground rules for these graduated and grown, yet dependent, young guys.

Thanks in part to some more experienced friends who helped us break ground in this new area of parenting, we arrived at the following guidelines:

**\* You're welcome to stay.** It was important to let our adult children know how very much we loved them, and while they are now of "legal age" to get an apartment, to live in a dorm, or live away from home, they are also welcome to stay, as long as they are respectful and considerate of our family and home rules.

**\* We're happy to help.** We offer free board and room as long as they are committed, full-time students, free use of utilities, and home-cooked meals. If they don't go to college, we expect them to pay monthly room and board. This is more than fair and the only sure way to encourage maturity and their preparation for an independent future.

In today's world, most decent apartments demand hundreds of dollars in monthly rent. Then there is the issue of locked-in leases, transportation, car repair, and insurance, not to mention, coin-eating laundromats, furniture, household items, TV, microwave, phone fees, and grocery supplies. All in all, living at home with mom and pop, even when paying room and board, is a far better buy than what the outside world demands.

**\* In return we expect.** Our teens and grown children are expected to work, even during a busy school year, at part-time employment. It builds character and assures them of the spending money they need.

My friend Mary advised, "Part-time jobs not only gave our kids the money needed to pay for their expenses, it gave them a healthy and committed work ethic. They were always coming home with words of praise, good pay raises, and even a few awards, from employers who appreciated what good workers they were."

"This attitude didn't just happen," she suggested. "The kids learned early the importance of being on time, keeping a commitment, seeing the value of steady work, and reaping the benefits through pay. More importantly, they had a feeling of accomplishment."

**\* Curfews, courtesy, and checking-in.** During high-school years, we strictly enforced an 11:30 to midnight curfew — extending it only for special dances or activities. Even then, late-night fun was off limits on school nights and permission was to be sought before attending any event.

For those out of high school, however, curfews are self-imposed, unless there is a consistent pattern of abuse. We ask instead, that they keep "reasonable hours," not later than 1:30 A.M., and no staying out all night or "half the night." By this age we believe their own good judgment and self-discipline should help them to set proper limits on their socializing so as not to interfere with college and part-time work schedules, as well as the family's right to respectful hours. "If you have trouble knowing when to come home we'll step in and tell you," my husband told the boys. On occasion, we have had to do just that.

The first summer after graduation, Tim just couldn't seem to remember when to come home. He had a summer job that wasn't too demanding, bought his first car — a snazzy, little number — and he had a cute girl whose parents were more lenient on late-night hours than we were comfortable with.

After warning him several times, we grounded him for two weeks and took away the keys to his car. Was he shocked! It was almost like he had been given too much freedom all at once.

It took just two well "grounded" incidents of parental encouragement and Tim was back on track.

In another vein, we insist that our young adults "let us know," as a matter of common courtesy, if they do not intend to be home for supper, are going out for the day or evening, and (approximately) when they will be returning.

We want our young adults to know that our home must never be treated like a flop house or "pit stop" between events. If "checking in" is asking too much, then the adult child should reconsider his or her plan to remain at home and check-out before tempers fray.

\* **Basic ground rules never change.** While curfews and constraints may change as youngsters grow to young adults, some basic ground rules in a Christian home should never waver. In our home these are:

*Love God.* Unless their employment or a special event conflicts, we ask that our adult children join us for Sunday Mass and (when home) evening prayers. This sets a good example for younger brothers and sisters. More than that, we sincerely believe that the "family that prays together stays together." On the Sunday or Holy Day when the young adult is unable to attend with the family, he or she is expected to go on his or her own.

*Honor thy father and mother.* Our home is "Our Castle" and our faith and values, are deserving of respect. Rudeness, violence, disrespect, vulgar and abusive language or inconsiderate behavior is not tolerated.

It goes without saying that a parent should never feel intimidated or humiliated by a grown child. Such behavior dishonors the parent and encourages a child, at whatever age, to become a tyrant and bully. If a young adult cannot control himself or demonstrates disrespect, or worse yet, abusive behavior, he must move out.

*Drunken, abusive, or promiscuous living is not allowed.* For the young adult's sake, as well as the parents, who would be forced to stand on the sidelines and mourn, a young person must not be allowed to pour through the door in a repeatedly drunken condition.

Likewise, if a child is openly living a life of sin by adultery, fornication, or addiction, (even if not done in the home), he or she must leave so as not to mock and scandalize the faith and values of the parents. The tone set by the oldest children in a family will not only leave an impression with the ones to follow, but parents who permit a child to openly live in sin are by their silence condoning the behavior. Young adults are free to choose their own faith and standards, but as long as they are living with their parents, they must abide by the parents standards.

\* **Pitch in and help.** The parents offering their love, home, and security during these transition years, have a right to ask that adult children at home "pitch in" and do their part. Even when a young adult is paying board and room, the parents or home must never be treated like a "live-in-and-got-a-maid" arrangement. Helping with laundry, keeping their room clean and presentable, and doing weekly chores to lighten the workload is a MUST and most assuredly the best way to show gratitude, affection, and love.

Christ Himself was the best example. He lived obediently with His parents, Joseph and Mary, until age thirty when He began His public life.

As a mom to many I've learned that when it comes to tidy rooms or housecleaning, daughters can be just as sloppy and thoughtless as sons. My friend Dorothy, a mother of two college-age daughters, finally resorted, after repeated pleadings and warnings, to imposing a $25.00 fine for a bedroom "that wasn't neat and presentable or when weekly chores were neglected." Laura, one of the daughters (now twenty-four and married), laughingly recalls, "I lost $100.00 that first year, but I did learn."

No parent wants to be reduced to berating and nagging. If by age eighteen a young man or woman is not considerate enough to respect the parents right to a neat and orderly home, an imposed fine is more than reasonable — and perhaps the only uncomfortable reminder which prods the child to helpfulness.

* **Signs of independence.** A full-time college student should be earning enough in wages to pay for his or her own gas, clothes, transportation, supplies, and treats. Otherwise, even the most passive of parents will come to resent a "Freddy the Freeloader" who takes his or her parents' support for granted.

Mike, a father of young adults contends that "self respect, freedom, and true maturity only come to those who earn it."

"Once our kids began to pay for their own luxuries, necessities, and incidentals, they came to recognize a kind of 'grownupness' they had in comparison to the former high-school chums they saw who were not paying board and room and 'living off mom and dad.' "

* **Light housekeeping rules.** The use of the telephone, television, appliances, and family car is not an

automatic given when it belongs to someone else. An adult child should ask, as a matter of respect and courtesy, before using his or her parents' equipment.

Our home, like many, would be thrown into utter chaos if we set no standards as to the use of the phone and TV. In addition, with the presence of little ones who would follow like those behind the Pied Piper, we feel it all the more crucial that our rules forbidding day-time TV, trashy soaps and movies, or endless hours of even the "best" sitcoms be honored.

\* **The telephone.** Phone calls at our house, with some exceptions, are limited to ten to fifteen minutes. Anything longer must be worth a quarter and a trip to the phone booth at the local shopping mall. This, too, demonstrates respect for other family members as well as those on the outside waiting to "get through."

\* **Dorm kids, returnees, and vacation times.** Students or young adults coming home, whether for temporary holiday vacations, during a job transition, or personal crisis, should expect to share in the day-to-day chores and responsibilities of the family. Parents do themselves AND their grown children a great disservice when they do it all "for them" and take on the role of servant or caretaker. This attitude will hardly encourage maturity, responsibility, and self-esteem.

Anne, a mother of three college and adult-age children said, "When Clark came home for Christmas his first year away, I thought it would be a wonderful time for all of us. Instead, we had three weeks of friction because he returned with the notion that 'I'm now a guest and no longer have to pitch in.' Until we got that straightened around, all of us were unhappy and frustrated."

Sometimes adult children who come home to live think their presence is a favor and welcome nostalgia to the parents. No thought is given to lost parental privacy, the intrusion, or invasion caused, unless the air is initially cleared and early guidelines established.

\* **Setting a departure date.** Some parents find it

necessary to set goals and a date of departure for their grown children in order to encourage a healthy "moving on" rather than an unhealthy interdependency.

Angie and Ron, parents of four grown children, found themselves with two sons in their mid-twenties, both of whom had lucrative careers, yet were still living comfortably at home. "One morning," Angie recalls, "after the boys had spent another late night out and were *sleeping in*, Ron got up and said, 'That's enough of this. We need our privacy.' He woke both boys up and told them they had until the end of the month to find their own place to live.

"We wanted some order and privacy in our lives and an end to the late-night returns," Angie said. "The boys found an apartment nearby and all of us are happier and closer."

Our family, like millions of others, is learning that the building of solid family relationships comes ONLY through communication, mutual respect and a willingness to work at it. The growth into adulthood after high school can either be a time of breaking or bonding — depending upon the attitude and commitment of both parents and child.

With prayer, grace, and love, the years ahead with our young adults will be a time (even through those "lumpy" and difficult periods), that we can look back on as one full of blessings and perhaps a specialness that truly worked to cement the ties that bind.

165

## Chapter 26

# How Do I Know It's Love?

"How do I know if it's love, mom? I mean, how did you know with dad?" asked my twenty-one-year-old daughter in as casual a manner as she could.

"Can you tell when a feeling is for REAL or when it's something that will pass with time?" she pried.

Perhaps she was asking because she and her "steady" had gone together for a year (a milestone in her datebook) and feelings were running deep. Or, perhaps my Chrissy was just vocalizing the age-old concern of millions of other young women and men: "Is this for keeps or isn't it?"

"I don't have a pat answer to the 'Love question,'" I told her. "Every individual is different, and so too every marriage. No set formula applies for everyone."

In my folks' case, my mother delights in retelling her own love story of how she met my father. Never mind that out of fifty-four years of marriage, they battled through at least fifty-three and one-half of them. In mom's mind that first kiss created such ecstasy, just the mere *recollection* of it, would inspire her and ease her through another fifty-four years of wedded madness. To each his own. In my own case, it was the budding of a wonderful friendship. I felt a comfort level and a freedom I felt with no other man. I could laugh with him and be myself. He was my confident and my buddy. Unlike my mom's feelings with dad, however, there was no "bell-ringing" first kiss.

It wasn't the romance or sexual attraction that hooked me on my "Polish Prince," although handsome and charming he certainly was. No. It was his genuineness, his homespun unpretentious manner, and his gentle and unassuming desire to know and be with me that won me over. He was my friend first — lover later.

"How did I know it was love?" I said in response to Chrissy. "I can recall one evening in particular, several months, maybe six, after we started dating. Up to that point I had never given marriage serious thought. Oh, I visualized what it would be like with others, but the vision was always faulty.

"This particular day, I was getting ready for John to pick me up and as I stood canvassing my closet for just the right outfit, I suddenly asked myself, 'What would my life be like if there were no John to look forward to?'

"No John? My heart sank. I realized for the first time that I wanted him in my life FOREVER."

Not long after my discussion with Chrissy, our son, Charlie, (age nineteen) came home, and announced that he was engaged. We had met the young lady (age twenty-two) only twice and very briefly. They had known each other for little more than two months, but Charlie was SURE it was love. So sure and so eager, in fact, that they bought a diamond ring and charged it with her credit rating. They planned to marry, he explained, in approximately three years when he has graduated from college.

Knowing this was his first serious girlfriend, and realizing he had three years of school remaining, and no present job, student loans to repay, and virtually nothing by way of courtship experience, we were not overjoyed.

We pleaded with him to give it time. "Please slow down. If it's really love, it will only grow stronger." we unsuccessfully begged. "We will pray for you, Charlie, but we can't offer our blessing on something so rushed into," his father said.

Charlie left a very unhappy fellow.

Later that evening, Chrissy and her younger brothers, Tim (nineteen) and Tony (seventeen), came in offering their own ideas and uncertainty — an interesting twist coming from siblings who always stick together. And yet these young people had read the danger signals, too.

To Tim, just the thought of a permanent commitment and marriage had him shaking his head and saying, "Man, this teaches ME something. I better back off with my own girl. I'm not ready for that stuff." Interesting!

In talking things through, I told them of my friend Diane's daughter Janice who was engaged twice to two different fellows. Each time she initially thought, "This is it," and each time, within a period of six months or less, she realized it wasn't right. "During that engaged process Janice came to realize that their fundamental beliefs and values were worlds apart. More to the point, her strong physical attraction in each instance, weakened with the passing of time."

Janice hit on the crux of why some marriages fail. It's not sex. It's not lack of communication or excitement. And it's not money, although these all may play a part. No. It's a basic difference in fundamental values and beliefs. If one believes in the permanency of marriage and the other does not, trouble lies ahead. If one believes a strong faith life is essential and the other does not at least offer respect and support, dissension will quickly take root. If one believes in fidelity, children, and mutual sharing and the other does not, the marriage is doomed.

"Was Janice immature?" I asked my threesome. "Not really. It took a special maturity and courage on her part to break off the wedding plans before she found herself locked into a miserable marriage."

When Janice finally met "Mr. Right" she was 25, an older and wiser person, and this time she KNEW. She also brought to her beloved the cherished gift of her sexuality — something she had reserved for her future husband.

"Janice, like a majority of young Christians, knows that sex outside of marriage is not only a clear violation of the Sixth Commandment," I explained to my unusually captive audience. "It also denigrates and diminishes the sacredness of matrimony itself. This commandment is one of love and protection to insure fidelity of the spouses and to strengthen their marital union. It is also meant to insure that a child conceived as a result of sexual intimacy will be born into a loving, committed, forever family — something that is NOT present in an unmarried relationship."

It was time to talk "turkey." Some of their friends had already "made some mistakes" with pre-marital sexual involvement, and realizing that my own kids are not immune, I felt compelled to let them know that **it's never too late for chastity**. And it's never too late to practice chastity or to bring it to your marriage. When you do, you bring to your marriage a personal, emotional, physical, and spiritual plateau you share with no other.

Back to Charlie. After much discussion, we got into the, "Is it love?" question. To our delight and mutual surprise, we and our young adults ended up in a lively discussion on the meaning of love. Here are some of the differences between love and infatuation we pointed out to them:

* **Impetuous versus prudent.** The infatuated person has "fallen in love." There is a breathless, head-strong, impetuousness that seems to say "I can't wait, we're so in love." Underneath is a strong current of anxiety and mistrust which fears the beloved may slip away if you wait.

With love, there is a purposeful desire to be prudent and an awareness that it "didn't happen overnight." There is a peaceful sense of surety and certainty — "Of course, we'd like to get married now. But we can wait."

* **Passion or friendship.** Infatuation is built on chemistry — the sexual attractiveness of the other person. The urge for physical intimacy takes center stage in the relationship.

With love, the friendship was established first and then comes the desire for intimacy. You can have fun just being together. You are friends first — lovers later. A good question to ask is "Would I choose this person for a friend?" or "Would I enjoy being with this person as much if it were someone of the same sex as myself?" In most instances the answer would be "No."

* **Ego over other.** Infatuation makes you feel like you've "landed the big fish" (the football hero, the girl everyone else wants, etc.) and that alone makes you over-

look differences. Love brings comfort and ease, never a bragging, boasting, or "look at my catch" attitude. Love would never reduce the other to an achievement.

* **Self before other.** Infatuation causes one to think of his or her feelings first. A sense of urgency and self-gratification ("I want it now.") is hard to stifle.

With love, the good of the other is foremost. No actions or plans take place that would jeopardize the other's reputation, future, or peace of mind. Love leads you upward. It makes you strive to be a better person.

* **Insensible versus sensible.** Infatuation often causes a loss of appetite, an inability to concentrate on studies, work, or personal affairs. Perhaps this is where the phrase "love sick" came from. When it's love, however, the person feels secure and eats, sleeps, studies, and works with renewed vigor and determination. There is a desire to do well for the sake of the loved one.

* **Isolation versus family and friends.** Infatuation can cause the couple to isolate themselves from family and close friends. There is a built-in fear of disapproval, even if no one has raised an objection. A sure clue that it's infatuation and not love is if friends and family disapprove.

With love, you feel an eagerness for family and friends to meet your beloved. You want them to know and love your chosen just as you do.

* **Closed-mindedness versus openness.** In infatuation, you overlook things you would never tolerate in an ordinary friendship, i.e. the person's drinking, abusive behavior toward others, sloppiness, lack of personal or religious standards. Passion blinds you from seeing the REAL personality of the other. It also causes a tendency to be short-tempered and intolerant of family members and friends who may, out of concern, point out the pitfalls of your relationship.

When you're in love, you have taken the time to know the other, and are aware of any shortcomings. You are also appreciative of those who offer counsel, such as in the case of differences of faith or perhaps a recovering chemical dependency. With love, differences are never minimized, but rather are discussed with a determination to work together to overcome any areas of concern.

* **Incompatible versus compatible.** With infatuation, you're usually uncomfortable discussing issues of fundamental values, including perhaps politics, religion, or social concerns. The slightest probing may result in more conflicts than similarities.

When you're in love, while you may be opposite in personality there is an openness, acceptance, a willingness to bend, and a sweet tolerance of the other's thoughts and feelings. Your fundamental beliefs and values are the same.

* **Foolish versus futuristic.** With infatuation, you may find yourself doing things you would never otherwise approve. Those things are justified as "okay" because you're in love. Little thought is given to consequences or the future.

With love, you want the best for your mate and you want to BECOME the best in his or her eyes and the eyes of others. Thus, you will guard against any careless, selfish, or thoughtless temptation which could undermine your mutual goal to be together.

* **Insecurity versus trust.** With infatuation, you feel sure of the other — as long as the other is near. When you're apart, there are feelings of uncertainty ("I wonder if she really had to study tonight" — "Is he really working late?"). Jealousy, suspicion, and an inner fear of having it all come to an end prevails. A flirtatious gesture or innocent invitation by an outsider causes distrust and insecurity. With infatuation, you're never really happy or secure.

When it's love, you have an inner peace that tells you that your beloved is yours, no matter what may temporarily separate you. Where infatuation is jealous and resentful, the person in love trusts. There is never a fear of infidelity because you know he or she is committed to you.

* **Today versus tomorrow.** With infatuation, you think of little else but the "here and now." Feelings are uppermost and your eagerness, restlessness, and jittery an-

ticipation make you miserable when you're apart. Yet, a future together is unclear, and (if you are honest) full of misgivings.

Love brings a feeling of security and a sense of nearness even when the loved one is away. You want to be together, but you know she or he is yours and you can wait. Love is patient and confidently makes plans for a future together.

When you're in love, you carefully prepare for the kind of home, family, children, and lifetime you want to share together, recognizing the responsibility needed in order to offer security and a future to the other. St. Paul says it best in 1 Corinthians 13:4-8:

"Love is patient, love is kind. It is not jealous, [love] is not pompous, it is not inflated, it is not rude, it does not seek its own interests, it is not quick-tempered, it does not brood over injury, it does not rejoice over wrongdoing but rejoices with the truth. It bears all things, endures all things. Love never fails."

What is the verdict in Charlie's case? Is it love or infatuation? Only Charlie holds the answer. We don't doubt his feelings nor his sincerity. If it's really love, time is on his side.

# Chapter 27

# Unwanted Labels

If I could launch a national campaign for the cause of my choice, it would be to wipe out the idea of the "unwanted child." I can't think of a more repulsive notion.

What will our children and future generations to come think of a society that labeled some of its children with such a sign of total rejection? More important, do we want children today growing up with the notion that there is such a thing as a human being — in fact, usually a tiny, defenseless baby — that is so inconvenient, so unplanned, so imperfect, or so unlovable that he or she is better off dead?

My father quit school at age sixteen. As the oldest son of seven children, he learned early how much his Italian immigrant parents needed help in providing for their family. My mother, the second oldest in a family of ten, speaks little about her memories of the Great Depression, except to note that "nothing was ever thrown out."

How did our parents live through such troubled events and manage to project hope and a feeling of being wanted to their children, even when they came at the worst possible times?

I came into this proud, work-oriented family, as did my two brothers, not by birth and blood lines, but by adoption. We were made to feel special, chosen, and very much wanted.

Perhaps it is peculiar to my upbringing, but I cannot recall even one incident in the course of my growing-up years when children conceived during the bad times were referred to as unwanted. In fact, I never knew that there was such a person.

There were labels for some children. Those born with

physical or mental disabilities may have been negatively categorized as "not quite right," "abnormal," "unfortunate," or worse. Although these descriptions are reprehensible, they are a far cry from a tag branding a child so grotesque or undesirable that his very existence is threatened.

In those days, no one was viewed as so unredeemable as to be regarded as completely unwanted.

Today's talk of "unwanted children" reminds me that I and those like me were once unplanned, inconvenient, untimely, and unquestionably stressful to our birth mothers. Were we anything else, there would have been no need for our adoption.

Still, we grew up in an age when adoption enjoyed the old adage: "Adopted and twice loved."

"Twice loved." That is, once by our birth mother who gave us life, and again by our adopted family who embraced us as their own.

While the unwed mothers of that era most certainly faced stigmatization and shame, the child became a welcome, if not cherished, member of society. We were an "answer to many years of prayers," my mother so often told my adopted brothers and me. We believed her.

What we didn't know was that adoption agencies back then had far more adoptable infants than they did eager parents. Today the reverse is true, with most prospective adoptive parents facing a five- to ten-year wait or turning to foreign countries for a baby.

Whatever happened to "adopted and twice loved"? When did we turn from a nation that cherished and protected mothers and babies, even the unplanned, to one that promoted the loveless, violent act of abortion?

If all of us who are adopted could speak out, I believe we would begin by reminding abortion advocates that we are no different, no less human, and no less deserving, just because some of us were conceived in drunkenness, anger, or less than loving circumstances.

Maybe in fact, life is all the more precious to us, because we know the slim thread of love that held us intact in our mother's womb. Adoption, in my mind, has always been a great act of unselfish love.

Some of us were the result of runaway love, incest, or the violence of rape. We know that. Nevertheless, we are grateful to God for our lives, and to our birth mothers whose sacrifice brought us into being.

Thank God for the unselfish birth mothers and perhaps birth fathers and grandparents, who relinquished their own immediate hopes and fears, in order to give us life and a promising future through adoption. I'm here today because of them.

Where would I and so many thousands of others be had abortion been sanctioned by law, as it is today, and OUR birth mothers surrounded by the same type of hard sell: "It's quick, it's safe, it's legal, and it's your 'right' (read duty)" propaganda? It takes little imagination to answer.

I've come to realize that we and our birth mothers had a chance that today's unwed pregnant women and their babies do not: The freedom to choose LIFE, instead of the pressure to submit to abortion.

Contrary to years past, today's unwed pregnant women are told little about adoption. It's not pushed. It's not promoted. It's not advocated. It's not even talked about.

Abortion today is portrayed as the kinder "solution," while "giving up your own flesh and blood" through an adoption plan, is tainted as the worst of all possible choices. Dismemberment and death has become the compassionate solution.

In decades past, we have striven to be that nation eager to offer hope to the hopeless and life to the burdened. No child was so disease-ridden, so handicapped, or troublesome that we did not seek to overcome whatever hurdle existed to offer him or her a decent future.

Will our children say of us that our solution was to destroy the diseased instead of the disease? Will they confess that we used our technological tools, like amniocentesis and ultrasound, as lethal weapons to weed out any suspected "imperfects"? Will they wonder what intrinsic value they have and if that value might change should they become disabled from an unforseen accident?

Our intolerance is all too apparent when they hear such talk about the "solutions" to the problem of "unwanted children." What a label to grow up hearing.

What must our children think as they view our diligence at saving the seals, working for conservation, and animal rights, while our apathy and silence promotes the "freedom to choose" to kill babies by legal abortion?

What a stigma to pass on to our children, i.e. "You were wanted, dear. Abortion is only for those 'unwanted' kids."

And what message does that tell the adopted kids of today? I already know the answer. It came from my black-skinned, Asian-born son who was airlifted out of Vietnam after witnessing the demise of his whole family. One day he announced out of the clear, "I'm sure glad I wasn't born in America, or they might have got me, too."

My son, born in the throes of poverty and cruel devastation, sincerely believes he was better off conceived in a war zone than inconveniently created in the richest, most powerful, most "peace-promoting" country in the free world.

There should really be no such label as an "unwanted child." For those unwed mothers unprepared for parenting, perhaps it's time we adopted kids end our silence and speak out: "For the sake of your already living unborn baby — choose life. Choose adoption. It's a great act of unselfish love. Take it from those who know."

# Chapter 28

# Breaking The Barriers
# To Special Needs Adoption

One of our children's all-time favorite "made-for-TV" movies is *The Orphan Train*, which beautifully depicts the story of a New York missionary woman who devoted her life to find adoptive families for the city's homeless children.

After feeding, clothing, and tutoring the orphaned waifs, she would escort them by train across the states in search of eager couples who heard of her work and wanted to adopt one of the youngsters in her charge.

The story was particularly meaningful to this household because seven out of fifteen of us are adopted. Like the young in the film, many of our children were "older," or classified to be of "special need" because of age, race, and physical or mental condition.

Though every adopted child's "story" is unique, the film was a charming portrayal of "love in action" and a reminder that adoption is God's OTHER way to create bonds and build "forever" families.

So successful has it proven to be, in fact, that until quite recently, most Americans saw adoption as a good and noble thing to do — and "in the best interests of the child" when difficult circumstances warranted it. Reflecting that sentiment were laws and attitudes, formed from public opinion, which came to recognize the adopted family as entitled to the same rights and privileges as those genetically related.

In addition, it was the religiously sponsored organizations and agencies that were in the forefront, offering aid to pregnant women and support for the concept of adoption.

* **Times have changed.** Instead of going forward, however, we seem to be sliding back. There exists today a not-

so-subtle, "anti-adoption" attitude which has created a climate in which abortion or "keeping the baby" is portrayed as the more acceptable (if not "loving") "choice."

An exaggeration?  Let's consider:

* The Center for Disease Control estimates that nearly a million and one-half to two million abortions occur EACH year — twenty-five percent or more of which are repeat abortions. Thousands of women have had three, four, and five abortions.

* Each year, of the hundreds of thousands of unwed pregnant teens who carry their pregnancy to term eighty-five to ninety percent will quit school and become single parents, rather than choose the option of adoption.

Why? The reasons are varied, complex, and in some ways disturbing: First, the increased availability, acceptability, and accessibility of abortion has been a leading factor. Pregnant women seeking guidance and direction often hear nothing more than "think of yourself FIRST" — get rid of the "pregnancy" and get on with YOUR life.

Second, the acceptance of out-of-wedlock pregnancies and the concept that single parenting is no longer viewed as misfortune but rather a "choice" has certainly had a profound effect.

One can only wonder how many thousands of babies were denied the chance for adoption because a young pregnant mom in distress was made to feel she shouldn't "give up her own flesh and blood." Many social workers today concede that "there are more older babies (one year or older) being placed for adoption than in years past" as single moms, after attempting to parent, seek a more secure life with two parents through adoption for their child.

* **Federal study reveals counselor bias.** Perhaps the most shocking report to appear is that compiled by Dr. Edmund V. Mech for the Office of Adolescent Pregnancy Prevention (OAPP), which reveals that the current anti-adoption attitude is caused in large part, by the very profes-

sionals trained to offer counsel and help, i.e. pregnancy counselors.

The federally-funded Mech study entitled "Orientations of Pregnancy Counselors Toward Adoption" reveals that "while a majority of counselors expressed positive attitudes toward adoption as an alternative to parenting" (forty-seven percent stated adoption was their personal preference), adoption actually ranked LAST or NON-EXISTENT (my emphasis) in the solutions these same professionals presented to their young clients. The reason according to the Mech study:

* "Few counselors believe pregnant teens want information about adoption."

* "The accuracy of counselor information was only about sixty percent." Approximately forty percent displayed an insufficient and inadequate knowledge of the subject.

* "Only about half (fifty-three percent) of the agencies reported setting any special qualifications for pregnancy counseling. Health facilities in particular were more likely to lack special requirements for counselors, especially those agencies with a high client-to-counselor ratio (100:1)."

* "Nearly forty percent of the counseling available to pregnant teens fails to include the adoption option."

Thus, in many cases, adoption is NEVER EVEN MENTIONED, and in the instances (some sixty percent) where it is spoken of by a pregnancy consultant, the information given may be insufficient or inadequate.

So much for freedom of choice.

It comes as no surprise that adoption is not promoted by Planned Parenthood-type, abortion-providing agencies. After all, abortion is their business. That and contraceptives seem to be their only business. They leave it to social welfare departments or adoption agencies to discuss the options of adoption or single parenting. They offer, in fact, no prenatal classes or adoption-support programs to a pregnant and panicked teen.

From abortion providers, we can expect pro-abortion counseling. However, when social welfare and adoption agencies themselves fail to even offer, much less promote, adoption, we should be outraged! What an abuse of authority for counselors not to present this choice when advising pregnant teens who are so troubled and vulnerable.

Most disappointing of all is the fact that many religiously sponsored adoption agencies now refer for abortion — treating it on equal footing as the options of "keeping" or making an adoption plan.

* **Adoption bias hits parents and children.** The situation has become serious enough to warrant U.S. Congressional hearings on the "Barriers to Adoption" and the steps needed to reverse the antiadoption tide.

And not a minute too soon. Most Americans are aware of the numbers of couples who wait years to adopt, the "waiting lists" backlogged for years to come, or those who adopt from foreign countries, because of the shortage of U.S. adoptable babies. Yet:

   * The plight of parentless children in New York City has received much media attention, including a *Newsday* story entitled, "The City's Other Homeless: Abandoned Babies." Little Alena was one amongst many hundred, who, not yet a year old at the time of the telling, was learning to walk on her crib mattress in the pediatrics ward at Lincoln Hospital in the Bronx. When Elena is old enough to climb the steel-barred sides of the crib, a top piece will be clamped on, "completing the cage." Alena, four-month-old Anthony, a baby known only as "Baby Girl," and two hundred other infants in New York City are tagged "Boarder Babies." They will live in these medical facilities until "appropriate" homes can be found.

   * Eric Brettschneider, New York's administrator of Special Services for Children, stated that for the

first time in years the city has allotted almost one and a half million dollars for congregate care beds (a modern term for "orphanages") to help ease the crisis situation of homeless children.

* Dorcas Hardy, former Assistant Secretary of Health and Human Services, stated at special U.S. Congressional hearings on "Barriers to Adoption" that there are at least thirty-six thousand parentless children in America. In addition, there may be one or two hundred thousand others living in foster or group home situations, children not yet free for adoption because of legal red tape or reluctance on the part of parents to terminate their parental rights.

The greatest obstacles to permanency and adoption for these "special needs" children (a large portion of whom are minority, older, or handicapped) are the courts' reluctance to terminate parental rights and social workers refusal to place adoptable minority children with parents of another race.

* **A call for a Christian response.** Not everyone will hear an inner call to become foster or adoptive parents of these infants, but we can all work to break down the barriers that keep these children parentless and others victims of abortion. How can we help?

First, we can pray for a recommitment to family and children in this country. Next we can support the National Committee for Adoption and other adoption support agencies that survive on charity and generosity. Finally, we can contact our state and congressional leaders, asking for legislative changes to help overcome the obstacles.

* **Civil rights act for parentless children.** We must call for passage of a Civil Rights Act for parentless children, whereby no child can be denied a permanent family if an agency-approved family is available. Present social policies deny adoption sometimes solely because of race, age, or condition.

The insistence by social workers that minority children be "color-or race-matched" to adoptive parents is a worthy goal. In reality, however, thousands of children may spend years in foster care because of such practices. Those with physical or mental disabilities or who are older have even less chance. There is a shortage of minority couples willing or able to adopt, so these children wait.

When we first applied to adopt in the early 1970s, we were discouraged because of the National Association of Black Social Workers boycott against white families adopting minority children. Ironically, it was only after three foreign adoptions (one of whom was Black) that we were approved to adopt a U.S. child. The youngster was Black/Caucasian, had serious physical and mental disabilities, and had spent her first two and one half years in foster care — awaiting a "racially-matched" family. We and she had thus been denied two and one-half years of love by the very "policy" that was supposed to offer her security, permanence, and identity.

* **Equality in insurance.** Adopted children in my home state of Minnesota are now guaranteed a right to the same insurance coverage as a child of like circumstance who was born into a family. Most states, however, provide no such guarantee — leaving potential parents and waiting children in a limbo, or worse, when it comes to the question of, "Will our adopted child receive adequate or complete insurance coverage?" They will if we support them and urge state legislatures to do the same.

* **End tax breaks for abortion.** Legislation is needed to put an end to giving tax monies to organizations that directly or indirectly provide, promote, or perform abortions. Laws must be reversed that demonstrate a public policy which promotes killing over caring.

We could begin by offering tax subsidies to couples who adopt children with severe disabilities (as is done in Minnesota).

* **Medical assistance.** We must care enough to call for passage of a catastrophic adoption subsidy or medical assis-

tance provision for those adoptable children with severe physical or emotional disabilities.

One mother told of her years of frustration trying to obtain financial assistance for her adopted daughter, who is profoundly limited due to cerebral palsy and other disabilities. The mother had intentionally postponed her adoption of the little girl for two and one-half years. She knew that once the child was legally adopted she would bear tremendous financial responsibilities. The ironies she described are experienced by many.

If the child remained a ward of the state, her caregiver would receive a monthly allowance, full coverage for all medical costs, and even respite care so the caregiver could take vacations or get a break. In addition, any home remodeling needed to accommodate the child (for a wheelchair or special bed) would be subsidized. None of this help was available to those who chose to parent by adoption for the child's lifetime.

Adoptive parents are like all other caring, loving, and committed parents. They are not miracle workers and they do not believe in hand-outs when they can manage themselves. On the other hand, there are situations with regard to adoptable children with special needs that are so catastrophic, so severe, so devastating to a family's financial security that it seems an act of mercy, if not one of justice, that they be offered some type of minimal aid when the burden becomes overwhelming.

The New York missionary woman in *The Orphan Train* reminded her critics of St. Paul's words (Romans 8:14, Galatians 4:25, Ephesians 1:5) that through a spirit of love we are "all children of God" and thus brothers and sisters.

To children, every day is a milestone. They are either reinforced daily in the knowledge that they are loved or they are scarred by the belief that they are "unwanted."

As "adopted children of God," Christians have a special "mission" to pray and to act for the love of Christ and the good of others. Let us call for an end to the social boycott that denies so many little ones what they need most during their impressionable growing-up years — parents, permanence, and love!

And let us, by our prayers and actions demand an end to the anti-adoption mind-set that has caused millions of babies death by abortion, and blighted the fabric of this great land.

185

# Chapter 29

# Most Mary Like

When Joseph, our thirteenth child was born, Johnny and I, and the rest of our energetic enthusiastic brood, were thrilled. After all, another of God's precious miracles had been given to our family.

I have to admit, however, that sometimes, amidst the diapers, dishes, dinners, and day-to-day demands of my family, I feel a bit overwhelmed and find myself asking: "How can my life possibly relate and identify with that of Mary the, Mother of God?"

Granted, Mary may not have enjoyed automatic washers, dryers, disposable diapers, an air-conditioned home and car, or an occasional lunch out with a friend. But neither did she have to worry about raising her child in a society filled with the temptations of R-rated movies; rampant sexual permissiveness and promiscuity; or materialism.

To put it bluntly, a friend of mine, bemoaning her daily challenges of mothering, not-so-kiddingly remarked, "The priest today told us to 'think of Mary,' but I told the Lord it's hard to relate to her. She had only *one* son and **He** was perfect!"

Many of us struggling through motherhood — whether it calls us to midnight feedings, nursing-on-demand, enduring the "terrible twos," or the growing pains of adolescents and teens — may experience the same sense of not being able to identify with the life and struggle of Mary. After all, we know that Mary was chosen by God and was indeed perfect in her own human nature and sinlessness before God. No one before or since can freely make that claim.

Perhaps if we contemplated the **real** life of Mary and not merely that which is portrayed so often in sentimental

Christmas paintings and pageants, we would begin to comprehend, better relate to, and pray to Our Blessed Mother.

In Luke 1:26-38, we read of a young, perhaps no more than fourteen years old, virgin girl who was betrothed to a man named Joseph. When the Angel Gabriel appeared to Mary, Luke tells us "she was greatly troubled at what was said and pondered what sort of greeting this might be." Without giving her much of a chance to sort things through, the angel went on to tell her, "Do not be afraid, Mary, for you have found favor with God. Behold, you will conceive in your womb and bear a son, and you shall name him Jesus. He will be great and will be called Son of the Most High, and the Lord God will give him the throne of David his father. . . ."

When Mary asked the angel, "How can this be since I have no relations with a man?" she was merely told, "The Holy Spirit will come upon you, and the power of the Most High will overshadow you. Therefore the child to be born will be called holy, the Son of God."

We have all read and heard these lines a hundred times. It would seem that Mary's first real step in faith must have come at that moment. She not only had to believe that she was talking to an angel of God, but also had to accept his message *solely* on faith.

After all, WHO was the "Holy Spirit" to this young Jewish girl? Believers today know through the Bible and Church tradition that the Holy Spirit is one of the three persons of the Holy Trinity. But this wisdom was not available to Mary.

Next, Luke tells us of Mary's great act of submission to God's will: "I am the handmaid of the Lord. May it be done to me according to your word."

I must confess, I would have either demanded more proof and details from the angel, or I would have been like Elizabeth's husband, Zechariah, struck mute by the shock of it all. In reality, is there any young girl, before or since Mary, who could have demonstrated such total trust in the angel's vague message? I can think of none.

This total submission in faith should be a great source of strength to both men and women of today who are called at times to blindly trust in God's divine providence.

The first real confirmation of the angel's words that we know of, didn't come to Mary until many weeks, or perhaps even several months, later while she was on a lengthy, and perhaps frightening journey (remember young single women did not travel alone in those days). She was traveling to visit her cousin Elizabeth, whom the angel had also announced to be "with child."

We can guess that this long trip was difficult for Mary. Besides being pregnant, unmarried, and traveling without a male chaperon, she may have been physically sick. Like any other expectant mother, Mary must have been subject to bouts of fatigue, nausea, and morning sickness.

Only when she had arrived at Elizabeth's door and was greeted by her cousin with the words, "Blest are you among women and blest is the fruit of your womb," did Mary have confirmation that the angel's words were true.

If Mary was hoping to hide her pregnancy until she was respectfully married, or feared the cultural punishment of the time — stoning — she demonstrated no such hesitation. In fact, she did the opposite, bravely proclaiming:

"My soul proclaims the greatness of the Lord, my spirit rejoices in God my savior, For he has looked upon his handmaid's lowliness, from now on all ages will call me blessed. . . ."

Mary's next act of faith came at the birth of Jesus. Certainly this humbling and bizarre event alone would have caused Mary to question the angel's previous "Good News."

Most pregnant women, even in Mary's day, had access to clean, pleasant, prepared, if not sterile (boiled water), surroundings to aid them through labor and delivery. If I had been Mary, delivering my baby in that stable or shelter, I think I would have challenged both God and man over the circumstances of my life.

As to the infant's birth in a barn, we can well imagine

what the REAL presence of farm animals must have been like — the smell of hay, tiny field mice, bugs, and ticks that hide in the "sweet hay," and the NATURAL aroma of spending the night with a shed full of chickens, cows, pigs, geese, ducks, and sheep. What an act of true faith it took for this brave, young woman to continue to believe that she was actually giving birth to the Son of God in such surroundings!

Although Mary did receive a reconfirmation of the Angel Gabriel's promise when the shepherds came to pay homage to the child, these first callers, who tended sheep in a nearby field, were hardly the town elite.

And, what must she have thought when the three Magi from afar brought with them gold, frankincense, and myrrh — items that were clearly identified by the Jews of that time with funeral and burial rites? Thus, with the kings' visit, Mary received her first clue that her newborn baby, the Savior of the world, was destined to suffer and die.

This is dramatically reconfirmed again, when Mary and Joseph took Jesus to the temple (The Presentation) for the ritual of purification, and Simeon, an old and pious man, declared through the power of the Holy Spirit, "Behold, this child is destined for the fall and rise of many in Israel, and to be a sign that will be contradicted and you yourself [Mary] a sword will pierce so that the thoughts of many hearts may be revealed" (Luke 2:34-35).

It's hard to comprehend what must have gone through this young mother's mind regarding the fate of her child. After all, she may have been sinless, but she was not God. She had no way of knowing what this "piercing" by sword prediction of Simeon meant, but it unquestionably was a dreadful foretelling of things to come. In spite of it all, Mary continued to trust God. Her example of faith in the face of uncertainty should give each of us renewed strength in time of crisis.

At the Finding in the Temple, Mary shows her humanness just as any frightened, Jewish mother would. To Mary and Joseph, Jesus was lost or kidnapped.

After a three-day, frantic search and journey, they finally discover their young boy casually teaching in the temple amidst the teachers, where "all who heard him were astounded at his understanding and his answers." Showing what a typical mother she must have been, Mary asked, "Son, why have you done this to us?"

How many times were similar words said by questioning, concerned parents?

In fact, most of us can picture our own fright and frustration. Yet, Christ's reply was simply, "Why did you come looking for me? Did you not know that I must be in my father's house?" His response brought no further scolding and interrogation. Again, Mary trusted.

Ironically, after this one incident of public attention, Jesus *obediently* goes back with Mary and Joseph, not to be heard of again until He is approximately thirty years of age. As Mary is our example of faith and trust, Christ is our model of obedience and love — love and obedience to His earthly parents and to the Divine Will of His heavenly Father.

The Wedding Feast at Cana is the Scripture scene I most identify with. Here is the Jewish mother who notices that the wine has run out and says simply to Jesus, "They have no more wine." She did not nag, elaborate, or coax. She made a simple statement.

Yet when Our Lord attempted to beg off from revealing His worldly mission by saying, "My hour has not yet come," Mary, like most mothers who live by intuition, would not take "no" for an answer.

How often in each woman's life do we intuitively sense what is best for our children, our loved ones, or the people around us? And, how often when we act on that perception do we, like Mary, though perhaps totally unaware, help perform little, everyday miracles by serving the needs of others?

Our Blessed Mother teaches us at Cana to "press" for the miracles — in our own life and in those around us.

At Cana, Mary did what most good mothers do when confronted with a negative reply by her Son. She ignored the response and instructed the head waiter to "do whatever he tells you."

Mary KNEW this was her Son's "hour" of exposure and the beginning of His public ministry. By then, she must have known too that her request of Him to perform a public miracle, would send Him on the road to the persecution, challenges, and the destiny that Simeon and the Magi had predicted so many years earlier. And yet, Mary, for the sake of her *other* children — you and me — prodded Christ to change the water into wine.

This Cana love — for the good of another, is an example for all of us to gently, yet firmly prod, encourage, and even require of our children or loved ones, the performance of good deeds, and acts of giving.

Mary, the Jewish mother who cared so much about those at Cana, is today our model of courage. While the world today preaches apathy, with its, "It's not my problem," or a "Do-nothing," non-involvement, Mary shows us selfless love.

Finally, at Calvary, after silently and powerlessly watching the torture, persecution, and ultimate "nailing to the cross" of her beloved and innocent Son, Mary comprehends Simeon's words foretelling her own "piercing with a sword."

Every mother and father who ever loved a child can imagine how painful and piercing this crucifixion must have been for Mary to bear. Any parent who ever sat with a child in a doctor's office, or a hospital's emergency ward can identify in a small way, Mary's agony and pain.

Finally, Jesus' words to Mary at the foot of the cross must have been almost bittersweet. In saying, "Woman behold thy Son," He refers not just to John, but to us. At the Cross, John was our stand-in representative. In this proclamation Mary is asked two things by her dying Son: to forgive His executioners, and to mother and love through eternity, all humankind — the very individuals who put her Son to death.

Could any of us turn around and mother and love the very ones who brutally tortured and killed our child? Not I.

Mother Teresa of Calcutta, India, has so often said, "If you've ever REALLY loved, then you know pain."

Mary certainly knew pain, and she, by her quiet consent to the Will of God, shows us firsthand that the Cross and love go together and are both God's gifts.

The concept of being "Most Mary Like" was often used a few years back to describe (usually) a woman who, by her manner and behavior, portrayed a miniature Mary to those around her. Unfortunately, that phrase is not in use as often today. Nor do we pray, as we should, for the grace to be Most Mary Like?

Mary is not just the ideal for women. Men — especially seminarians and priests, who profess a lifetime vow of virginity and celibacy — should be urged to see Mary as their model and their Mother. As priests do today, Mary consecrated herself body and soul to become a virgin vessel, who by the power of the Holy Spirit carried Christ to others.

Perhaps if we could envision that each one of us has been given a unique role to fulfill, we would attempt to become like Mary — a spiritual vessel bringing Christ to others — for the love of God.